I0035325

Setting Performance Targets

Setting Performance Targets

Carolyn Stringer
and
Paul Shantapriyan

business**expert**
Press

Setting Performance Targets

Copyright © Business Expert Press, LLC, 2012.
All rights reserved. No part of this publication may be reproduced,
stored in a retrieval system, or transmitted in any form or by any
means—electronic, mechanical, photocopy, recording, or any other
except for brief quotations, not to exceed 400 words, without the prior
permission of the publisher.

First published in 2011 by
Business Expert Press, LLC
222 East 46th Street, New York, NY 10017
www.businessexpertpress.com

ISBN-13: 978-1-60649-137-9 (paperback)
ISBN-13: 978-1-60649-138-6 (e-book)

DOI 10.4128/ 9781606491386

A publication in the Business Expert Press Managerial Accounting
collection

Collection ISSN: 2152-7113 (print)
Collection ISSN: 2152-7121 (electronic)

Cover design by Jonathan Pennell
Interior design by Scribe Inc.

First edition: December 2011

10 9 8 7 6 5 4 3 2 1

Printed in the United States of America.

Abstract

Targets are an important part of our work life, whether we are setting them or meeting them. Target setting forms part of the budgeting process and the performance management of business units and individuals. Unfortunately the behavioral impacts of target setting on performance are not well understood, and this can lead to serious consequences such as game playing. Target setting is an under-researched area.

Our aim in writing this book is to help fill the gap in target setting for performance. The pivotal issue in target setting is that it is an art as well as a science. Managers must strike a balance between understanding and working with the psychologies of the people undertaking the organizational initiatives and the science of estimating probabilities, preparing budget forecasts, conducting sensitivity analysis, and so forth. We do not tie down the reader with the narrow view of target setting but take a more holistic and richer perspective.

A feature of this book is that we draw on ideas and research across disciplines, which is rarely done in this field. Target setting is an under-researched area, as most of the research is on measurement and incentive compensation. This book fills the gap by drawing insights on target setting from a wide range of sources and across disciplines. Our book introduces the reader to some of the important methods, such as forecasting, sensitivity analysis, and probability analysis. We use practical examples to show how these techniques can be applied in target setting.

Our focus is on highlighting how interrelated the various parts of organizational activities are and how they impact on each other. Therefore, target setting must include an understanding of the organizational context (e.g., people, competitive environment, structure, strategy), as well as the impact of incentive compensation and information flows. From this broad background, this book examines key issues such as which targets to choose, how many targets, and the level of difficulty.

This book is ideally suited for managers and executives. It showcases the critical choices involved in the target-setting process and offers advice on how best to manage and execute it. Budgets are the most well-known organizational target-setting process, so we use lessons learned from budgeting to provide insights for developing other performance targets for financial and nonfinancial measures.

Keywords

Target setting, goal-setting theory, motivation, performance measurement, performance management, strategy, value creation, external and internal benchmarking, relative performance targets, forecasts, target difficulty, stretch targets, highly achievable targets, line of sight, objective performance evaluations, subjective performance evaluations, incentive compensation, capped performance targets, operational budgets, fixed budgets, flexible budgets, rolling forecasts, controllability principle, weightings, short- and long-term targets, activity-based budgeting, Beyond Budgeting Roundtable Group

Contents

CHAPTER 1

Setting Performance Targets

Introduction

When an archer aims at the bull's-eye, the target, the focus is on getting the arrow from the bow to the red circle in the center of target. This focus requires strength in pulling back the bow string, coordination between the dominant eye and arm with a judgment call as to the wind direction, and angle of the release. We can use the science of physics—the tensile strength of the bow, the aerodynamics of the arrow, and compensation for wind and gravity. Robin Hood knew little of this science but relied on the art and judgment of his craft. Clearly, even in archery, hitting the target is more than just will and effort, it is rather judgment, ability, and the likelihood of hitting the target under environmental conditions. This book discusses not only the science but also the *art* of target setting.

Figure 1.1. Hitting the target.

Target setting is pivotal to managing performance in an organization. Targets focus the mind of the manager to know what to aim for. The manager then works out how to move the business from where it is to achieve the future expectations. However, no single target perfectly captures all aspects of a business. Therefore, multiple targets are often used.

Virtually all companies set targets, which include multiple short-term targets as well as longer-term strategic targets. To optimize the use of targets, important choices need to be made: How do you set targets in light of changing conditions? Should you set targets using a top-down or a participative bottom-up approach? How difficult should performance targets be? How many targets should be set and how do you weight them? Target setting is *"more an art than a science."*[1] The *art* in target setting is in making a balanced decision between competing choices. The following example highlights the serious consequences when organizations make the wrong choices.

Consider Sears, Roebuck and Co.'s experience with target setting in the early 1990s. Sears set a sales target for its auto repair staff of $147 per hour. This specific, challenging goal prompted staff to overcharge for work and to complete unnecessary repairs.[2] Ultimately, Sears Chairman Edward Brennan acknowledged that this target had motivated employees to deceive customers. From the Sears, Roebuck and Co.'s experience, obviously maximizing the sales target per hour had a downside. The result was a fall in credibility from a customer perspective, with a falling reputation, a risk not anticipated when setting a single target.

Nordstrom, the fashion retailer known for its exceptional customer service, is another example where performance targets have caused significant problems. Employees were held accountable for difficult performance goals (sales-per-hour). Nordstrom was taken to court because some supervisors were pressuring sales employees to underreport the time they spent on the job to boost their performance to target. The cost for Nordstrom was over $15 million.[3]

Choosing the Target—Strategic or Operational

How do you choose the target? What is relevant? How frequently do you evaluate performance to target? These are some of the difficult issues you need to consider in setting targets.

As this book unfolds, you will see that certain targets or key performance indicators have operational importance, others have tactical importance, and still other targets will have strategic importance. While targets that address operational efficiency are important in generating profits, it is essential to ensure that these cost-cutting targets do not result in loosing profitable customers. For example, a water company in the United Kingdom tried to find ways of reducing costs and one way was to outsource the call center. This would reduce costs by $10 million and therefore would increase valuable cash flows by $10 million. Unfortunately, this cost control target did not endear the water company to the customer. Customers balked that the overseas call center struggled with their regional accents. Customers were now switching away from the water company, and the likely loss was in excess of $75 million. Clearly, exceeding the operational target of cost reduction had a strategic consequence that needed to be addressed. The call center was then in-sourced back into the United Kingdom, and there was no longer a cost saving but rather a cost increase in the call center as the water company listened to the customers. The moral of the story is the importance of identifying core and noncore activities. The core activities and processes should not be targeted for cost reduction as they provide value to the customer. The key issue is to know what is strategically important and what to target at an operational level. This process requires a series of conversations between managers, support functions and the CEO to determine the right level for performance targets.

It becomes more difficult to understand what the relevant target is. You can paint red dots on every aspect of a business and expect the employees to hit the bull's-eye on every target. However, each numerical target does not always generate incremental value to the business. Take Mike, a marketing manager for a flour mill. He has been set a sales target of 200 tons of flour per annum. The regular customers are taking 175 tons a year at the normal retail price of $375 per ton. He knows that the cost of manufacturing the flour at the mill is $220 a ton. He thinks he can easily win new customers if the price is dropped. After all, the sales volume of 200 tons is the target. So when a rural township has a new fast food outlet that needs flour, Mike contacts them. As the cost of making the flour is $220 (or so Mike thinks), he sells the flour at $300 a ton delivered. He gets a three-year contract with them for 100 tons a year. Now clearly Mike has exceeded his target, but there is a downside. He has set the price without having a complete set of information. The cost of shipping the flour to the rural client is $100 a ton. This means that the flour now costs $320 to arrive at the rural township and the contract price is $300. The more that Mike sells, the greater the loss. This is an example of a target that gets the manager distracted from generating value to the business.

What may have been more useful to Mike is information sharing between the manufacturing depots, the logistics (transport), and the accounting function so that he had a more relevant target and the means to achieve that target. If Mike had been set a target that captured value generation, then he would have negotiated a price higher than $320.

A valid target is not just something that is easy to measure. There are several thousands of operational measures that are important to the manufacturing manager that, if frequently measured, analyzed, and reported, would pose problems. It is not uncommon to find that many operational measures used in organizations do not get reported.

As budgets are commonly used, this book draws on insights from target setting for budgets to draw implications for setting all performance targets.

Budgets: What Are They and What Use Do They Have?

A budget is a document that allocates resources for a future period. There can be several budgets in an organization: a sales budget, a production budget, a logistics budget, a capital investment budget, and a purchasing budget, to name a few. Each of these budgets will have targets. Therefore target setting is an integral part of budgeting. The overall purpose will be to estimate and match revenues and expenses for a future period, which can range from a month, a quarter, a year, three years. The longer the time line, the greater the uncertainties in estimating, matching, and arriving at a profit figure.

Let us look again at Mike. He has been given a target of 200 tons of flour. He has just won a new customer for 100 tons, boosting the total sales from 175 tons to 275 tons. Well done, Mike. However, that sales budget, a plan, needs to be linked to the purchasing budget. In this way, the purchasing officer can order the right type of wheat at the best price to meet and match the planned sales. The production budget, under the control of the production manager, needs to know when these orders are required. Then the logistics manager will include these plans into her budget so that the total delivery schedule is on time to meet and exceed the customers' expectations. Now the production manager states that by exceeding the 200 tons limit, the company needs to invest in new technology so that the business can expand its operating capacity. This investment needs to be evaluated quickly so that the new customer of 100 tons is not lost. It is clear from this discussion that a budget is a series of interrelated components.

Budgets are used for a range of purposes including planning, coordination, resource allocation, and motivation. A budget is also a plan for the future, it addresses the needs of regular customers, new customers, and strategic initiatives that will ensure the performance targets are reached. A budget coordinates and allocates resource between departments, functional groups, and support staff. The accountants, credit department and the IT department need to provide and maintain the back office functions necessary to keep the front line staff in touch with their targets. A budget therefore communicates, be it in financial terms (dollars and cents) and nonfinancial terms (tons, grade of flour, time to delivery).

Let us revisit Mike and his other senior managers. The production manager is upset that a lot of his time is taken up with writing up his capital budget request for a new machine. His concern is the 9 months taken to process his request for machines to raise the capacity from 200 tons to the required 275 tons. The logistics manager voices another sentiment. The time taken in all this budgeting process does not allow her to focus on her job, which is logistics. The business is likely to lose valuable customers if the budget does not integrate the operational budgets of marketing, manufacturing, and logistics departments. The overall aim is to deliver the flour to the new customer.

The time in preparing the budget is often up to 6 months. Taking so long to plan and implement a budget that may be out of date as soon as the managers leave the room is a recipe for confusion and bad decision making. One way to shorten the time frame is to set targets using last year's numbers and make adjustment for some changes (e.g., oil, currency). This reduces the time taken to forecast, plan, and coordinate. What can happen is that the coordination needed when the operational activities are integrated is missing because managers have conflicting objectives. For example, Mike needs 275 tons of flour for his target while the production manager's budget target is based on last year's budget scaled down by 5%. This common approach to budgeting that uses last year's numbers is flawed. For example, new machines are needed, which can only increase the production manager's costs. It is not surprising that, when results are different from the budget, no one trusts the budget.

Another way to shorten the budget time line is to reduce the line items without realizing the impact on value to the customer. Certain activities are strategic necessities to the business. The traditional thinking has been to use last year's costs to set future targets. Instead, each manager needs to identify key activities that drive value for customers. The budgets then need to reflect the resources required for these key activities. These resources are then forecasted and placed in a budget.

Budgets can also be used for motivational purposes. Motivation levels can be high if employees see the targets in a budget as highly achievable. When managers and employees are committed to the targets in a budget, they need to receive regular updates on performance, and believe that the targets can be achieved. In some cases, the quarterly and rolling budgets will provide baselines to measure unit performance. In other words, if a budget is achieved for that quarter, then clearly the signs are that the business is going according to plan. This performance management mechanism is one way in which an organization can control and direct activities within a business unit.

Using targets for motivational purposes requires an understanding of the importance of line of sight. Let us go back to the archery example. What happens if the archer, when pulling back the arrow and aiming at a target beyond their normal capability (a stretch target), finds that the target is obstructed because a person is standing in the way? The archer cannot hit the target directly and so aims the arrow above the obstruction, hoping to hit the target board, without any clear line of sight to hit the bull's-eye. Even Robin Hood would struggle to hit the target without a clear line of sight.

Line of Sight

Line of sight is important to motivate employees to meet their performance targets. This concept of line of sight came from Vroom's expectancy theory, which states that an employee is more likely to be motivated if they can see a relationship between their actions, the target, and the rewards for reaching the target.[4] Employees must have the ability to influence or control activities to achieve the set target.[5]

In many organizations, employees and managers are often asked to hit a budget cost target or market share target. Yet, they cannot see clearly how their actions could result in hitting the target. Take the example of a business unit manager who is asked to hit a stretch profit target. This business unit has 35% of the total cost structure being based on head office cost allocations. Then upstream business units, still part of the same corporation, are charging a further 28% of the bottom line through transfer pricing arrangements. Clearly, the manager's line of sight is obscured by corporate charges as well as transfer pricing. All this manager can see is less than 50% of the target, which is controllable.

Sometimes budgets occupy too much time and this distracts managers from what is important (e.g., customers). To perform well you need to know your customers. Targets are important for directing performance. However, focusing solely on the budget can distract managers from what they need to do to perform well. Do you focus your energy on setting targets for photocopying? Are you precise in this photocopying estimate to the nearest cent? If so, do you know who the top 10% of your customers are? Sometimes a business spends too much time on estimating photocopying expenses without knowing from where their wealth and value comes. We elaborate on customer analysis in chapter 6.

The key elements of target setting to improve performance include[6]

- making sure employees understand how their performance is being measured;
- training employees so they understand what they need to do to improve the performance to targets;

- recognizing how different levels of performance relate to rewards and punishments;
- providing them with regular information on performance to targets so they are able to make changes to improve performance;
- ensuring employees are empowered to make changes necessary to improve their performance.

Outline of the Rest of the Book

Setting targets is a crucial part of the budget process as well as organizational performance management.[7] Despite being an important issue, there has been little research and practical guidance on how to set targets.[8] This book provides an overview of key issues that executives and other managers need to know about setting targets for budgets and for other key performance indicators (KPIs).

Budgeting is conducted across all parts of an organization. The importance of budget targets to ensure financial performance is achieved is the focus of chapter 2. The design choices made in the responsibility centers of an organization (e.g., profit center) impacts on managers' accountability and responsibilities for budget targets. Budgets serve a range of purposes, such as coordinating, providing communication channels, planning, controlling, and motivating. The short-term operational plans must integrate with the future-orientated strategic plans and capital expenditure plans. It is important to understand the way the budgets are used to influence managers' behaviors.

Target setting in light of changing conditions is discussed in chapter 3. Traditional fixed budgeting, standard costing, and variance analysis processes are explained, along with the option of making the budget more flexible by taking into account the impact of volume changes or updating the budget forecasts more regularly (e.g., rolling forecasts). Traditionally, organizations have used objective comparisons to performance targets, primarily financial measures. To overcome problems with the objective evaluations (e.g., controllability), some organizations are taking a flexible approach by allowing more subjectivity in evaluations, such as taking into account events outside a manager's control and other factors not included in the objective performance targets.

The different ways to set performance targets is considered in chapter 4. Benchmarking is gaining in popularity. Ideally targets should come from external benchmarks that compare to the best in the industry. If you have no competitors, data is difficult to obtain, or you want to differentiate yourself, you need to develop internal targets. Relative performance targets are growing in popularity but care needs to be taken the benchmarks are fair. Other choices for setting targets include top-down, bottom-up participation, negotiation, and ratcheting. Forecasting and zero-based approaches can be inputs into the target-setting processes.

How difficult performance targets should be depends on the purpose of the targets as discussed in chapter 5. Target difficulty for motivational targets is very complex. Goal-setting theory shows that specific and challenging targets are better than vague statements like "Do your best." Olympian targets can work as directional signals but are not motivating if they are perceived as being unattainable. Setting targets that are perceived as unattainable can result in tension, stress, and game playing. Budget targets are typically highly achievable and offer a number of advantages for organizations and managers (e.g., more commitment, lower control costs, less gaming). Capped targets motivate managers to continue to increase performance when highly achievable targets are set. The purpose of the targets helps to determine how difficult they should be. For example, motivational targets should be highly achievable by the hard-working managers while forecasts should be set at the level of the expected performance for the purposes of planning.

Using multiple targets with a combination of financial and nonfinancial measures is examined in chapter 6. The reasons for the growing popularity of multiple performance targets include that they capture more aspects of performance and can include a mix of lead and lag measures. Important choices have to be made in terms of which targets to select, the number of targets and how they should be weighted. Understanding how the choices made influence people's behavior is crucial to effective target setting. Targets may not operate independently and there may be diminishing returns.

To address long-standing criticisms of traditional fixed-budgeting systems, two innovative approaches to change budgets are discussed in chapter 7. Activity-based budgeting may provide the missing link between operations and the balanced scorecard. In contrast, the Beyond

Budgeting advocates argue that budgets should be abolished and replaced with a new management philosophy. In practice most organizations are changing their budgeting systems by making regular revisions, including subjectivity in performance evaluations, taking into account only controllable factors, and using rolling forecasts.

The final chapter 8 provides an overview of the key issues in setting performance targets we have discussed in the book.

CHAPTER 2

Budget Targets

Show me the money.

—Cameron Crowe, *Jerry Maguire*

Introduction

In today's aggressive corporate board meetings, more than one director might growl "Show me the money." While Cuba Gooding Jr. in the movie *Jerry Maguire* captured the essence of challenging a manager, we have heard this often from directors. The real issue is that directors have to send financial signals to the stock market and investment analysts. The bottom line is the bottom line. All the great strategic initiatives, products, or service developments have to show improvements to the bottom line, be it in the short term or the long term.

This chapter focuses on budget targets because they are used across different parts of the organization. Operational budgets serve a range of purposes in organizations, including coordination, communication, planning, control, and motivation. The operational budgets are short-term plans, and it is crucial that they are integrated with the longer-term strategic and capital expenditure planning processes. The final point discussed here is the importance of understanding how the system is being *used* by managers in organizations, rather than its technical design.

Budgeting Is a Process Involving Multiple Levels of an Organization

The first issue to consider is the organizational structure because budgets are prepared for all parts of an organization. The organizational structure sets out who is responsible for each part of the business, where the accountability lines are drawn, and the boundaries for each budget. The responsibility and reporting lines are also designed to promote vertical communication and horizontal communication across the organization.

For a person to be held responsible for an activity they need to have the power to change one or more aspects of that activity. Take the example of Mike, the marketing manager for the flour mill discussed in chapter 1. It would be unwise for Mike to be responsible for the cost per unit of the product. How can Mike, the marketing manager, be responsible for the unit cost of manufacture when he has little power to influence the manufacturing process? This relates back to the concept of line of sight, elaborated on in chapter 1. In Mike's case he agreed to a contract price at $300 per ton for flour without communicating with the other areas of the business. Mike's decision, made in isolation from the other parts of the business, meant that he had committed the flour mill to making a loss on the new contract. This highlights the need to ensure clear vertical and horizontal information flows and communication lines between the various business units and the head office.

To keep it simple, we focus on decentralized organizations. Responsibility centers are a key part of decentralized organizational structures, as they define what activities a business unit is responsible for (e.g., to generate profits). Organizations may have four basic types of responsibility centers:

1. *Cost centers* can be engineered or discretionary. Engineered cost centers are often used for manufacturing units where product costs can be estimated reliably (e.g., direct materials, direct labor). Discretionary cost centers include such units as research and development and marketing. Clearly the activities of discretionary cost centers are not easily traced to products or services.

2. *Revenue centers* are where the unit is responsible for the generation of revenues (e.g., marketing departments).

3. *Profit centers* are used where the business unit focuses on the profit generated rather than merely the costs of products or services.

4. *Investment centers* are where profits are important as well as capital invested.

The type of responsibility center impacts on how the budget responsibilities are allocated. For example, the performance of profit centers is evaluated on profit (revenues less costs). Now this is a relatively simple exercise if the business units are fully independent and do not work closely with other internal business units. If the operations of the business units are closely interrelated, transfer pricing for the interbusiness unit transactions is required. The situation is even more complex for investment centers whose operations are closely interrelated because of the shared assets involved. Even if investment centers are independent, issues may arise about how to measure the return on capital invested, the cost of capital (e.g., Economic Value Added [EVA®][1]). For example, how should investment centers be evaluated if they have old assets that are fully depreciated but functional (the value of the asset base is close to zero), compared to other business units who are using the latest technology? Another issue is how to structure the head office support units (e.g., accounting, information technology). Should these support units be cost centers, profit centers, or investment centers? The structure needs to be considered when setting targets to ensure that the targets are reliable and relevant to the business unit.

The typical budgeting process revolves around the responsibility centers that support vertical communication processes in decentralized organizations. A problem is that this focus on vertical communication processes is incompatible for organizations that have flat or network structures or organizations that focus on integrating across the value chain (e.g., suppliers and customers).[2]

Operational Budgets Serve Multiple Purposes

It's clearly a budget. It's got a lot of numbers in it.

—George W. Bush

Operational budgets are short-term plans that are used for multiple purposes including coordination, communication, planning, control, and evaluation. The operational budget needs to match the organization's responsibility structure (e.g., profit center, cost center) and is based around providing line-item detail on revenues, expenses, assets, and liabilities. The focus of operational budgets is usually the next year.

Operational budgets can be developed in different ways. For example using internal targets (such as using prior period costs) or external standards (such as comparison with competitors or industry baselines). The different ways to set performance targets are discussed in chapter 4.

Coordination and Communication

Two of the purposes of budgets are coordination and communication. For example, the sales manager (responsible for the sales plan) would need to coordinate with the production manager (production plan and production capacity), the purchasing officer (inventory policy and material purchasing plan), the human resources manager (labor hiring and training plan), and the chief financial officer (the profit-and-loss statement, cash flow statement, and balance sheet).

Figure 2.1 illustrates how various parts of the operational budget (also called the master budget) are related to each other for a manufacturer. The organizational goals set the (1) objectives for the budget. The (2) sales plan links to the (5) production plan, the production plan links

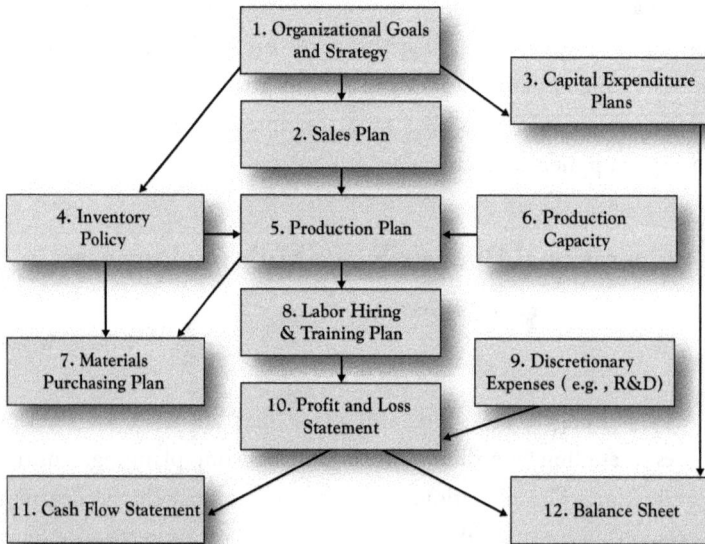

Figure 2.1. Elements of budgeting for a manufacturer.

to the (4) inventory policy, (6) production capacity, (7) materials purchasing plan, and the (8) labor hiring and training plans. There are also (9) discretionary expenses such as training, research and development, advertising, and (3) capital expenditure plans. Then the production plan, the labor requirements plan, and discretionary spending link to the operational budget, which includes the (10) budgeted profit-and-loss statement, the (11) budgeted cash flow statement, and the (12) budgeted balanced sheet. Budgets force information sharing horizontally and vertically across an organization.

Horizontal Communication and Coordination

The budget is a key coordinating device, as each responsibility center manager participates in the preparation of the budget. The budget also coordinates the resource allocation process horizontally across the business and support responsibility centers. For example, sales plans for the shipment of goods need to be coordinated with the production plan to ensure bottlenecks are avoided. The budget process enables people across an organization to identify inconsistencies between budget items that cross business areas, such as expected volumes, and production capacity. The budget is more than just financial numbers and also can include nonfinancial information on volumes and sales prices.

Does it matter if different responsibility units (e.g., marketing, operations) suffer from a lack of coordination? Let us return to Mike, the sales manager from chapter 1. He had to meet an increased sales target. He has booked sales of 275 tons, and the production manager has to increase the production plan to meet this sales volume. Now let us assume that the production manager decides that the sales plan is pure fiction and unachievable. He sticks to the 200 tons as his production plan and estimates costs this way. The result is that when the two plans are integrated, the profit-and-loss statement will use the production costs (based on the production manager's estimate of 200 tons) and the sales revenues for 275 tons (Mike's estimate). The result is an unusually high budgeted profit. The business is going to do really well! When the year is part way through, as more flour is produced, the actual profits are far lower than budgeted. Is it that the budget is at fault as it is historic and outdated? No, this was the result of the lack of coordination of the budgets between marketing and operations. This situation occurs in an organization when there is a lack of communication and coordination of the budgeting process between the head office and the business units.

The reason for the lack of coordination is that often managers control their own fiefdoms; they distrust the budgeting process and consider that the numbers are spun out without being grounded in reality. At the end of the period when the budget is analyzed and the variances computed, the common argument is that the budget is a poor reflection of performance.

Vertical Communication and Coordination

Coordination and communication channels up and down the organization are also important. Poor vertical communication and coordination can lead to problems. Managers may find the budgets for their business unit being set by the head office or by consultants, an approach that can have several consequences. Managers may feel that the numbers are unrealistic and unachievable (chapter 5 develops this further). Also, managers may not take ownership of the targets, and there might be a lot of pressure on achieving budget targets, leading to tension and stress. Another consequence is that managers may feel that the budget constrains their actions, and this may result in managers not seeing opportunities to be innovative.

By allowing business unit managers to participate in the budgeting process it is more likely that these targets will be achieved. One reason is that managers who have participated in the budgeting process are more likely to be committed to meeting the targets. This is because they understand how the targets have been formulated and what they need to do to achieve the targets. Another issue is that participation is necessary when some of the risk associated with meeting the budget targets is shared with employees through incentive compensation.

Budget participation at lower levels can also encourage people to develop new ways of doing their job better. Take the example of David, a senior executive who was struggling to meet the budget for his bakery. The bakers talked of bread being wasted as the hot bread was pushed into bags, resulting in crushed bread and wasted bags. One employee suggested a scoop that a rival bakery used, which contained and shielded the bread while the bag was pulled over the bread, running over the scoop.

This minimized the bread damage as well as the tearing of the bag. The cost of the new scoop was minimal at $250,000 for the machinery. This shows how grassroots ideas from employees to reduce waste and improve processes can help with meeting budget targets. This is the essence of total quality management. Logically, this bottom-up approach to improvement should also be the essence of the budgeting process.

The downsides of allowing people to participate in budget targets are that they may push for easy targets to be set or attain more resources than they need, leading to reduced organizational performance. Therefore an important issue to consider is how much participation should be allowed in setting the budget targets. We elaborate on participation in target setting in chapter 4.

Planning

Planning is a future-orientated process that forces you to think ahead and plan for different scenarios that could occur and how to respond to reduce risk. Planning is improved as each business unit plans and reports on the scope of its operation for the year ahead. This also means that the budget plans communicate what the business unit is planning to do to top management and other business units. The budget plans also integrate current operations (business as usual), with expectations of new customers, along with strategic actions that are going to be implemented in the next year. When the operational budgets for each area are integrated into the organizational budget, then you can tell if an *expectation gap* exists between what the business units say they can achieve and what top management wants to achieve. To be useful for planning purposes, operational budgets need to be set at what is expected to be achieved (see chapter 5 for further discussion on target difficulty).

Planning targets can be improved by using the experience of senior managers. Take the example of Dave, a senior executive in marketing, at a global steel manufacturing company. During recent restructuring, an outside consulting firm is brought in to establish targets and forecasts. The consultants and senior executives of the steel company did not interact much. The result is targets and forecasts that are confusing to the senior executives as they are the outputs of statistical models. The first problem is that the senior executives did not participate in setting the sales targets. A second problem is determining joint probabilities. Some customers would buy the more profitable steel products only if they could get the less profitable products as well. The statistical model developed by the external consultants and imposed on the senior executives did not take into account joint probabilities for the demand function across different grades of steel. The result was a set of targets that Dave did not think were feasible or realistic. He and other senior executives just shrugged their shoulders and went on with business as usual. Had the senior executives participated in the target-setting and modeling exercise, not only would the targets be realistic and achievable, but the motivation and commitment to the exercise would have been high. Employees can provide useful insights into the business operations that external consultants may not be aware of.

Control

The budget is one of the primary control tools used in organizations. Once approved, the budget sets out clearly what a manager is responsible for and the performance target that must be reached and to which he is accountable. The budget assists top management in monitoring performance to targets. Top management uses budgets as a control tool by analyzing variances to targets, with exception reports to focus only on deviations from what is expected (this point is elaborated on in chapter 3). While budgets are important for top management to control operations, they are often criticized as being a *command-and-control* tool, which places most of the decision-making authority at higher levels and focuses solely on short-term actions (e.g., cost reduction) rather than creativity and innovation.[3]

A problem with using budgets as a control device is that budgets can quickly become outdated. This is the reason why organizations are using more flexible approaches to target setting, including using flexible budgets (adjusted for change in volumes or other key drivers) or rolling forecasts (see chapters 3 and 7) and using relative targets (see chapters 4 and 7).

Motivation

The budget is the benchmark against which performance can be evaluated and rewarded (e.g., bonuses, promotions). Budget targets are used to motivate people to improve their performance. People perform better when they are given clear and specific performance targets that are not too easy or too difficult. We discuss goal-setting theory and how to set targets for motivation and evaluation purposes in chapter 5.

We have outlined that budgets can be used for coordination, planning, control, and motivation purposes, but which purposes are most important is up for debate. While most of the research has focused on motivation and evaluation purposes, a recent survey of Australasian companies finds that budgets are more important for planning and control.[4]

Conflicts

Problems are likely to occur when there are conflicts between the different purposes that budgets are used for. For example, how difficult should targets be in order to be useful for a number of competing purposes (e.g., planning and motivation)? Targets used for coordination, planning, and control purposes are best set around *what is expected* to be achieved. Whereas targets used for motivation purposes have some degree of *stretch* to encourage performance that is greater than expected. We elaborate on this point in chapters 5 and 7.

The next issue is that operational budgets need to be connected to the organizational strategy and the desired future direction of the organization. If the operational budgets are disconnected from strategic planning, resources can be allocated to the wrong areas.

Short-Term Operational Budgets Need to Integrate With Future Plans

Operational budgets are not just a standalone activity, they are the short-run element of the forward-looking processes that include strategic plans and capital expenditure plans. After all, if a budget indicates that the present strategy cannot be met, then the current strategy needs to be stress tested. A number of questions need to be asked: Is this strategy achievable? Does the strategy reflect where the business should be right now? Can this business afford to take that market position? The operational budget needs to be aligned with the organizational strategy (see the Astoria case discussed later in this chapter). The final point is to assess how the strategy links to the financials, that is, "show me the money." If these questions are not answered adequately, the espoused strategy becomes a set of clichés. The operational budget becomes a historic document that arrives late in first quarter and sits in the bottom drawer until the year ends. Management has already made their decision and completes the variance reports just to be left alone. There is often little evidence of learning from or stress testing the strategic implications of the budget.

Let us go back to the example of Mike, the marketing manager. Mike secured a new contract, which meant he exceeded his target of 200 tons by 75 tons. The production manager is now concerned, as the production capacity for the year is around 200 tons. To enable Mike to deliver the 275 tons he sold, production capacity needs to be raised. However, the production manager cannot deliver this quantity. What is an operational issue becomes a strategic issue because of the need for capital investment to boost capacity. Therefore, operational budgets can have implications for strategy. Another issue is whether this increase in sales would result in a head-on clash with the market leader? Clearly, an operational sales budget can lead to a strategic price war with a Goliath in your industry if operational budgets are not integrated with strategy.

A critical challenge is to ensure that operational, strategic, and capital expenditure plans are integrated. If different people are held accountable for different things, then it can be difficult to integrate and coordinate the plans. One option is to establish a head office group who is given the responsibility for the strategy implementation, coordination, and integration across the various activities (e.g., strategy development, alignment, operations, capital expenditure).[5] In this manner, a strategy that requires investment in new technology can see the appropriate capital expenditure planning in place, and this can assist in identifying potential synergies across the organization. This process would ensure funds available to implement the strategies or could identify that the proposed strategies could be difficult to implement.

Operational budgets are used to implement the short-run part of the long-term strategic plans.[6] The strategic planning process would normally include revenues and expenses and some low-value capital items. The range of strategic initiatives or programs can be diverse. Some programs may involve continual improvement programs, while others take the organization into new directions; some strategic programs require extensive capital expenditures, while others do not. For each strategic initiative some estimates need to be made for a range of costs (e.g., establishment, operational, and capital costs) and expenditures. These costs usually have different time horizons (e.g., incurred in the next year or the next few years).[7]

Strategic programs that require large capital funding are usually taken through the capital expenditure planning process. The capital expenditure plans are future-oriented and focus on large capital expenditure requirements that are linked to the strategic plans. Senior managers typically identify specific initiatives they wish to implement over the next 1 to 5 years (or longer). These capital expenditure programs may be organization-wide or linked to organizational or business unit strategies. The development of these large capital expenditure plans may involve preparing financial plans and using techniques such as net present value, payback, and internal rate of return. However, in many cases the potential outcomes of projects are qualitative and unable to be quantified. Often the success or failure of a proposed project depends on the negotiation skills and the political power of the champions of the project.[8]

There are three points to consider when integrating the operational and strategic plans: avoiding a short-term focus, allowing time for strategic initiatives to be implemented, and ensuring the visibility of the strategic plans when integrated into operational budgets. First, avoid taking a short-term focus in strategic planning. This requires a separate process to track strategic uncertainties that are significant enough to attract top management attention or to look for new products, services, or other developments that can dramatically change the competitive environment. The aim is to question, challenge, and debate key assumptions of why and how the business competes. Change the current strategy, if necessary. The iPhone and related products are good examples of what happens when competitors are not focusing on leading-edge technologies and so have to play catch-up.

The second point is to ensure the time allowed for strategic initiatives is adequate. The risk of failure increases greatly when short-time horizons are given for long-term strategic initiatives.[9] The pressure to deliver can result in managers rushing into new markets they do not understand, increasing research and development spending faster than can be properly managed, acquiring companies too quickly without integrating them into existing operations, and rushing into joint ventures without understanding the needs and motivations of the other parties. Strategy needs to be implemented incrementally and managed step by step.[10]

The third point is to ensure that the financial numbers for the short-term part of the long-term strategic plans remain visible in the operational budgets. This visibility of the financial numbers for each strategic initiative is important to evaluate how performance targets have been achieved. Any evaluation of performance raises a set of important questions. How has the good financial performance been achieved? Has this financial result been the result of cutting advertising, slashing repairs and maintenance or delaying resources for the launch of a new product or service? For example, turnaround expert "Chainsaw Al" Dunlap was famous for achieving spectacular short-term performance by his aggressive cost-cutting approach at several companies including Sunbeam, but his actions had serious long-term consequences.[11] A *McKinsey Quarterly* survey reports that 45% of organizations have failed to measure and monitor the progress to financial and nonfinancial targets for their strategic plans.[12] This may help to explain why organizations report that successfully implementing strategies is a major challenge.

However, it is one thing to design a financial system. How you use it is another issue.

The Design Versus the Use of a System

The budgeting processes, for example, can be seen as a defined set of rules and it is usually assumed that once designed, the budgeting system will work the way the designers intended it to work. However there is evidence to suggest that the way the budgeting system is designed to work may not be the way it actually works in practice. One of the problems is that often head office staff create a technical *masterpiece* and then prepare numerous pages of notes on how to use this system. The result is that creativity can be driven out, and it becomes an exercise in checking off boxes, without people committing to the process.

Budgets can be used to influence managers' behaviors in different ways. Argyris first drew attention to the distinction between the design of budgets and the manner in which the information is used.[13] His field study indicated that supervisors used budgets as "pressure devices" influenced by their view that subordinates are basically lazy and find work distasteful (a practice Taylor termed "soldiering").[14] Argyris found that the employees experienced greater frustration and job-related tension, and their fear and mistrust of supervisors also increased. The employees even formed groups to combat upper management. Such behavior would result in deteriorating performance. Research suggests that this situation is not uncommon. A high reliance on performance measures to budget targets for evaluation purposes can lead to job-related tension, social withdrawal, and strained relationships with superiors, which often results in manipulative behaviors and budget slack.[15] Therefore, placing a heavy emphasis on budget targets in performance evaluations can have negative consequences for the organization. A more flexible approach would be to take into account other factors in evaluations (see subjective evaluations in chapter 3).

Budgets can be also used in different ways operationally or strategically. Often budget targets are the focus of monitoring and control systems. The result is that managers can end up fire fighting, while strategic issues get little consideration. Case Capsule 2.1 provides an example of how budgets can be used operationally and strategically (e.g., continuous budgeting) to identify challenges and opportunities. Astoria is a large multinational organization, a real-world company given a fictitious name.[16] Primarily based in the United States, Astoria is a leading player in the global technology sector. Astoria has a relatively flat matrix structure with business areas organized functionally (e.g., research, intellectual property) and geographically (e.g., Europe).[17]

Case Capsule 2.1. Budget Targets Being Used Operationally and Strategically

Astoria operates in a rapidly changing business environment with high levels of uncertainty, rapid technology change, and continual innovation. The continuous budgeting process has been designed to encourage adaption and strategic change. The focus is on setting performance targets for a few critical factors and regularly monitoring them. Although there is no direct link between achieving individual targets and rewards, all rewards are linked to achieving company profit and the few critical strategic drivers.

The traditional view on variance analysis is to focus solely on performance to predetermined targets and take corrective action. Such corrective action tended to be short term and operationally oriented. Astoria now looks at problem solving and seeks strategically aligned responses. Astoria uses a range of techniques including process improvement, "story boards" that display performance measures, performance gaps, and the action plans. Integrating quality processes with budgeting encourages problem solving and improves learning across the organization. Performance to budgets is regularly monitored, but Astoria's managers also focus on identifying strategic risks and opportunities. Problems are solved collaboratively. The process here involves continual monitoring so that targets and strategies can be reprioritized as conditions change. This is an example of a budgeting process being used strategically.

The focus is on achieving Astoria's strategies, not on meeting the operational budget. There are trade-offs for strategic actions, for example, balancing the cost of delaying a new product launch compared to the cost of launching on time. Analyzing the potential alternative actions involves considerable discussion about what actions need to be reprioritized. While the case highlights budget flexibility, the managers were still required to meet the overall budget target. To meet the budget targets the managers were expected to make changes in other parts of their operations to offset the additional expenditure incurred on strategic initiatives. In Astoria's process of continuous budgeting, despite pressures on managers to meet the preset budget targets, they still can put a case forward for budget revisions.[18]

Summary

Budgets are seen as time consuming, retrospective and often the domain of accountants. Why should busy managers occupy their time in being part of this non-value-added activity called budgeting? The reason is simple: You drive the business, and therefore you should drive the budget. Let the budget be relevant to your needs and make sure your short-term operational plans integrate into the future-orientated strategic and capital expenditure planning processes. At the end of the day, organizational performance comes down to "show me the money."

Comparisons to budget targets are key ways that responsibility and accountability are exercised in organizations. Operational budgets help in coordinating activities across the organization. They assist in communication processes across the business units and up to top management. The budgeting process forces everyone to plan ahead and think about how their activities need to coordinate across the other business units. Regularly monitoring performance to budget is one of the primary control tools organizations use. It is also important to understand the way the budgets are used, rather than focusing on the technical features of the budget.

Key Learning Points

- Budgets are prepared at multiple levels in organizations. Responsibility centers establish who is accountable for budget targets and where the boundaries are.
- Budgets are used for multiple and sometimes conflicting purposes, such as coordination, communication, planning, control, and motivation.
- Operational plans are the short-term part of the future-oriented strategic planning and capital expenditure planning processes.
- The way the budgets are used influences managers' behaviors.

CHAPTER 3

Target Setting in Changing Conditions

Change is inevitable—except from a vending machine.

—Robert C. Gallagher

Introduction

Target setting faces challenges from changing conditions. A target is set, and subsequently underlying conditions change. Therefore, the target needs to be revised and the changes incorporated into the budget, or this will lead to poor decision making. The static approach where no change is recorded is called the fixed approach, while a more dynamic approach is called a flexible budget. We will illustrate the differences in these approaches by using two examples: one using a traditional fixed budget and the other using a flexible budget adjusted for the impact of volume changes. We also look at using rolling forecasts to capture the changing dynamics of the marketplace. We recognize that objective measures only partially capture the underlying value generation of a business and view subjective evaluations as a way of offsetting uncontrollable events. Now let us move on to fixed target setting.

Fixed Budgeting, Standard Costs, and Variance Analysis

In manufacturing organizations where there is a direct and stable relationship between inputs and outputs, it is possible to use standard costs to develop the budget. The standard costs may be developed from financial data or from engineered standards. Standard costing makes the budgeting process easy, as the budget can be calculated from the standards, taking into account any changes (e.g., increase in wages). Another option is to develop budgets using external benchmarks (see chapter 4). Standard costing also allows for tight control through variance analysis. The main problem with standard costs is that they only focus on costs, whereas other issues such as on-time delivery and quality may be more important.

Variance Analysis

Variance reporting is an attempt to update the fixed budget targets *after an event.* Having fixed targets provides a useful control mechanism and allows variance analysis (usually monthly). Variance analysis provides an important overview of the financial performance of the organization and can highlight good performance as well as acting as an early warning sign of potential problems (called exception reporting), as can be seen in the Case Capsule 3.1.

The main problem with variance analysis is that it only highlights certain areas to be investigated further. It does not tell anything about why actual costs are different to budget, how this has occurred, whether the problems can be fixed, and what action needs to be taken. Therefore variance analysis indicates the beginning, not the end, of an investigation. It is still focused on what has happened in the past and is not future orientated. If variance analysis is used monthly, then the budget needs to be split on a monthly basis. This can cause further problems especially where businesses are affected by seasonal variations.

The fixed budget approach is inflexible because if the organization has had a major impact on the budget early in the process, or if there has been an error in the budget, these items have to be continually reported on. We have sat in meetings when it looked like a business unit had made a massive loss, whereas this was just an error in inputting the budget figures (e.g., a line item recorded as a negative instead of a positive). The budget templates are often inflexible so that these problems and errors cannot be changed once they are loaded into the budget and need to be reported as variances each month. Changes in organizational structure can impact on budgeting, such as time delays before new account codes can be activated to reflect the new structure. Therefore, fixed budgets are only useful for organizations operating in stable environments.

Case Capsule 3.1. Springfield Marketing Department

The following example illustrates a traditional fixed budgeting approach calculated using standard costs and variance analysis of actual compared to budgeted costs for Springfield Marketing Department.[1] The budget is based on an estimated volume of sales of $500 million. It is easy to prepare line-item budgets (Column 1) where there are preestablished standard costs for different activities (Column 2), which allows you to easily prepare the budget (Column 3). By comparing actual costs (Column 4) to the budget you can calculate any differences between actual and budget, what is called variance analysis (Column 5). The variance analysis column shows that total budgeted costs were $225 million and actual costs were $245.5 million, resulting in cost overruns of $20.5 million. The variance between actual and budgeted costs of $20.5 million means that Springfield Marketing Department has overspent the budget.

Springfield Marketing Department

Standard costs*		Budget	Actual costs	Variance
Sales volume $500M		'000	'000	'000
Variable costs				
Sales Commissions	0.05 × $500M	$25,000	$32,000	($7,000)
Administration	0.02 × $500M	$10,000	$12,500	($2,500)
Supplies	0.02 × $500M	$10,000	$15,000	($5,000)
Travel	0.03 × $500M	$15,000	$17,000	($2,000)
Distribution	0.09 × $500M	$45,000	$47,000	($2,000)
Fixed costs				
Salaries	$52,000	$52,000	$53,000	($1,000)
Advertising	$27,000	$27,000	$26,500	$500
Entertainment	$12,000	$12,000	$11,500	$500
Maintenance	$9,000	$9,000	$10,000	($1,000)
Depreciation	$8,000	$8,000	$8,500	($500)
Supplies	$4,000	$4,000	$4,500	($500)
Insurance	$8,000	$8,000	$8,000	$0
Total Costs		$225,000	$245,500	($20,500)

* To calculate standard costs for Sales Commissions this is 5% of Sales.

Another issue is that variance analysis is often seen as the accountants' problem. With the time pressures of meeting month-end and year-end reporting deadlines, sometimes there is a lack of involvement by the business unit managers. Not surprisingly, business unit managers do not like variance analysis, as often factors are outside their control. Remember the case capsule on Astoria in chapter 2? Variance analysis should not merely look at differences between actual results and targets to enable actions to be taken; they should also ensure the decisions are strategically aligned. Strategies should be continually reprioritized as conditions change.

Flexible targets are useful if you have limited forecasting ability or are unable to make forecasts. The problem is that in periods of rapid change there is little historical data that can be used. We will now show how to make fixed targets more flexible so that you do not lose sight of the strategy.

How Can Fixed Targets Be Made More Flexible?

Flexible targets (e.g., flexible budgets, rolling forecasts) are useful to protect managers from factors that are outside their control. One approach is to recalculate the budget based on what managers are expected to achieve given the actual conditions faced during the measurement period.

Flexible Budgets

Flexible budgeting is the process whereby the budget numbers are revised to reflect the impact of subsequent changes in some of the key assumptions that underlie the budget, such as volume of the activity (e.g., sales, production), currency rates, interest rates, oil prices, or other factors.[2] This approach requires a good understanding of the cost-volume-profit relationships between key drivers of the business. Flexible budgets can be used to evaluate performance where volume drivers are important and where volumes are very difficult to predict. For example, they may be used by manufacturing managers who are held responsible for costs that vary with volume.[3]

A flexible budget may be geared to any level of volume and therefore can be based on the actual (as distinguished from the planned)

Case Capsule 3.2. Springfield Marketing Department—Flexible Budgeting

Let us go back to the Springfield Marketing case and recast it using a flexible budgeting approach. If you revise the budget using the actual level of sales ($600 million) and use this to calculate the standard costs, you get a very different answer from the fixed budget example in Case Capsule 3.1. You can see that the overall variance to budget is only $500,000 because the budget has been adjusted to take into account the actual sales volume of $600 million (not the $500 million sales budgeted for in Case Capsule 3.1). The actual variable cost line items are not too far away from the flexible budget. Therefore, the manager now can see more clearly which items need to be reviewed and what corrective action, if any, needs to be taken. This example highlights the importance of understanding the cost-volume-profit relationship and how using fixed budgets to evaluate performance can be misleading.

Springfield Marketing Department

			Actual	Flexible budget
		Actual sales $600M		variance
Variable costs	**Standard costs**	'000	'000	'000
Sales commissions	0.05	$30,000	$32,000	($2,000)
Administration	0.02	$12,000	$12,500	($500)
Supplies	0.02	$12,000	$15,000	($3,000)
Travel	0.03	$18,000	$17,000	$1,000
Distribution	0.09	$54,000	$47,000	$7,000
Fixed costs				
Salaries	$52,000	$52,000	$53,000	($1,000)
Advertising	$27,000	$27,000	$26,500	$500
Entertainment	$12,000	$12,000	$11,500	$500
Maintenance	$9,000	$9,000	$10,000	($1,000)
Depreciation	$8,000	$8,000	$8,500	($500)
Supplies	$4,000	$4,000	$4,500	($500)
Insurance	$8,000	$8,000	$8,000	$0
Total costs		$246,000	$245,500	$500

volume attained during the budget period. A thorough knowledge of cost-volume-profit behavior enables management to determine what costs should have been if we knew what actual volumes would be when we developed the budget. A comparison between a flexible budget for any responsibility center and actual results achieved becomes a reasonable basis for evaluating performance. Differences between planned and actual volume, which may not be within the control of the person being evaluated, are eliminated from consideration. The controllability issue is discussed later in this chapter.

Rolling Forecasts

Another way of dealing with uncertainty and focusing on strategic issues is to use rolling forecasts. The idea is to provide rolling forecasts for a few critical performance measures (e.g., sales, profits, cash flows), and regularly track performance to targets. The rolling forecasts are continually updated for the organization's critical performance measures and all cover the same period. These rolling forecasts are not linked to budget targets and rewards, so the problems associated with this are avoided. Rolling forecasts used as targets also have their disadvantages as there are time and cost considerations. We elaborate on forecasting in chapter 4, and rolling forecasts are an important part of the Beyond Budgeting approach we discuss in chapter 7. One of the Beyond Budgeting companies uses forecasts that are updated quarterly and are forecasted for the next six quarters (as shown in Table 3.1).[4]

Table 3.1. Rolling Forecasts: Six Quarters

	Year 1				Year 2				Year 3			
	1	2	3	4	1	2	3	4	1	2	3	4
First quarter												
Second quarter												
Third quarter												
Fourth quarter												
Fifth quarter												
Sixth quarter												

We now examine the issues with objective performance evaluations and how allowing some subjectivity provides flexibility in the performance evaluation process.

Objective Versus Subjective Uses of Performance to Target Comparisons

Performance to targets can be evaluated in an objective or a subjective manner. For example, an objective approach would be to focus on quantitative targets to assess performance. These quantitative targets may include financial measures (return on investment [ROI], return on capital employed [ROCE]) as well as nonfinancial measures (e.g., number of accidents per year). If the actual performance is better than expected, then the performance is rated favorably as a positive number or index. A more subjective approach, while taking into account performance to targets, would be to make adjustments for uncontrollable factors such as the impact of the global financial crisis. This adjustment may be made through a peer review by other managers at the same level, or by the senior management team.

Objective Use of Financial Targets

Objectively using performance targets generally means using quantitative measures in a situation where performance is specified at the beginning of the evaluation period. Financial measures are considered more objective as they can be independently audited, and the responsibility for measuring financial performance is independent of the process (e.g., the financial controllers are in control).[5] Furthermore, profit and the accounting numbers are often the language of shareholders, and therefore using such measures allows the business to meet external objectives. The final argument for using financial measures in performance evaluation is their "contractible" nature. This means that financial numbers can be used in a performance contract and can show why a manager did or did not achieve contracted performance targets. Therefore, it comes as no surprise that firms tend to assign a high weighting to financial measures in incentive compensation systems.[6]

Limitations of Using Objective Targets

There are a number of limitations when targets are based on objective financial and nonfinancial measures. The problems with financial and nonfinancial measures are well-known; they are often described as being imperfect and inaccurate because of measurement issues or the problems when measures are aggregated at the organizational level.[7] Financial measures, for example, are often incomplete as key dimensions of performance are omitted (e.g., improvements in personnel and product quality), and they can be misleading when examined at the organizational level.[8] Another issue with objective financial measures is that they are historic and backward looking.[9] Focusing on performance targets set annually causes managers to take short-term actions, as the outcomes of many managerial decisions, both favorable and unfavorable, are not evident until sometime in the future.

Another issue with using preset objective targets is that they may not be a good indicator of performance. It could be that the performance targets were set at a level that was too easy to be achieved, or the good performance has resulted from good luck such as windfalls from unexpected changes in currency rates, or it could be the result of gaming actions. Managers may have achieved the good performance results by taking a range of actions to meet their fixed budget targets. Some of the games managers play include pulling income forward from future periods by delaying expenses or increasing revenues when a target is not attainable, negotiating easier targets, and accelerating sales near the balance date to meet the budget target.[10] Alternatively it could be that poor performance has resulted from events that were outside the manager's control.

The Controllability Principle

Managers are often evaluated and held accountable for events over which they had only partial control.[11] This violates the *controllability principle*, which is based around the view that holding managers accountable for items over which they have little control and linking this to incentive compensation increases their risk.[12] If managers are not compensated for the additional risk they bear then the organization will suffer the costs of their frustrations, reduced motivation, and possibly greater management turnover.[13]

However, there has been considerable debate in the literature over the controllability principle. An alternative view is that managers should be evaluated on uncontrollable events because they have to deal with a number of factors that influence financial performance (e.g., market, economy, competitors).[14] The argument is that managers should not be protected from uncontrollable events if they can take actions to reduce the organization's exposure to losses.[15] Clearly, knowing and identifying which events are controllable or uncontrollable is important so that the use of objective measures remains valid. The following case capsule highlights the issue.

Case Capsule 3.3. Currency and Controllability

Robert, as a manager of a New Zealand business unit, sets a target to sell 1,000 sports car rims (18 inch) at NZ$1,000 for each set of four rims to Sharon's Car Mart, a client in California. The client at that time has translated the order into U.S. dollars at a rate of US$0.61 to NZ$1. At the start of the negotiations, Sharon thinks each set would cost US$610, which she can comfortably sell for $900. By the start of the new ordering season, the U.S. dollar has fallen to a rate of US$0.72 to NZ$1. This means that Sharon would now have to pay $720 for the same set of rims for which she had planned to pay $610. She thinks that the price hike of $100 per set of rims is too high, and so she switches sources. Now Robert has lost a sale of 1,000 sets of rims, and this lost sale is beyond his control. Therefore, his business unit sales are lower than budgeted and the profits are affected. In using the accounting numbers (e.g., sales in dollars, profit in dollars, return on investment [ROI]), the lost sales can be regarded as uncontrollable. Therefore, there is merit in taking away the uncontrollable elements from the bottom-line profit so that the manager is only accountable for what he can control.

However, are all these events uncontrollable, or could Robert have taken actions to reduce the impact of the currency changes? What would have stopped Robert from looking at a futures contract, hedge, or a foreign currency option? In this way, the U.S. client would not have to carry the risk of the falling U.S. dollar. The issue for debate is whether certain events are uncontrollable or whether the risk of such an uncontrollable event can be mitigated or managed. If a risky event can be mitigated, then the managers could be held accountable for a wider spectrum of events.

Research shows considerable diversity in the way the controllability principle is being used in practice.[16] Case study research often provides examples where the controllability principle is not used. Whereas a recent survey finds that 25% of the financial controllers in Canada adjusted for the effects of uncontrollable variables when the budget variances were being evaluated, and around 32% of the responding U.S. firms adjusted the budget numbers to take out the effects of uncontrollable events.[17]

To overcome some of the problems of evaluating performance relative to fixed and objective performance targets, some flexibility can be introduced by allowing subjective performance evaluations.

Subjective Uses of Performance to Target Comparisons

Subjective evaluations are becoming popular because they allow more complete evaluations of performance and can overcome some of the common problems with using objective targets, as discussed in the previous section.[18] The European Corporate Governance Institute recommends adding a subjective element to incentive compensation plans because this can reduce the risk to the organization and the employee from uncontrollable factors, windfalls, and gaming the system.[19]

Subjectivity can also improve the performance evaluation process when done by experienced evaluators. The use of subjectivity may also be more appropriate for senior managers who are used to dealing with ambiguity and complexity. For example, General Electric's CEO Jeff Immelt was evaluated in 2008 based on processes that included a mix of quantitative and qualitative performance measures.[20] Immelt's performance in 2008 was based on a subjective assessment of measures including revenues and organic revenue growth, earnings, earnings per share (EPS), cash flow from operating activities, return on total capital, percent margin, sustaining operating excellence and financial discipline, retaining an excellent team with a strong culture, managing the company's risk and reputation, building an excellent investor base, leading the board's activities, and stock price.

There are a number of ways that subjectivity can be incorporated into performance evaluation and incentive compensation plans, including[21]

- basing the whole incentive compensation plans on subjective evaluation criteria;
- using objective measures but with discretion over the choice and/or weighting of the measures;
- allowing subjective judgments to be made at the end of the financial year to take into account uncontrollable factors or other relevant information that has just become apparent;
- using relative performance targets and taking into account factors that have become evident at the end of the evaluation period (see chapter 4 and the discussion on Beyond Budgeting in chapter 7).

Some evidence shows that allowing subjectivity in evaluations is even more common than using objective performance to target comparisons.[22] Subjective evaluations linked to incentive compensation plans are also increasing in popularity.

Advantages of Subjective Evaluations

Subjective performance evaluations have numerous advantages including that they allow superiors to take into account other factors so the evaluation is more accurate and complete, as evident from the General Electric example earlier. Subjective evaluations could take into account a manager's ability to react to unforeseen situations or could make use of new information on market conditions, competitors, and so on that has come available since the formal objectives were set, to adjust for outdated targets.[23] Subjective evaluations can also filter out the impact of uncontrollable factors, as discussed earlier. Including a degree of subjectivity in performance evaluations may also help avoid some of the problems (e.g., game playing) with the use of financial measures, for example, by taking into account the impact on quality when managers take short-term actions like cutting costs. Subjective evaluations also provide some insurance to employees to minimise the risk of losing their incentive compensation payment due to uncontrollable events.[24]

Disadvantages of Subjective Evaluations

Subjective evaluations are challenging to implement properly. Often valid measures are lacking and a range of targets may form the basis of subjective evaluations. Some indicators are favorable to the subordinate manager while other indicators are unfavorable. The weighting of the indicators becomes a source for perceptions of unfairness. Subjective evaluations can also been seen as unfair and biased, and there may be game playing to improve ratings (e.g., favortism bias).[25] Research shows that superiors often find it difficult to give bad news in evaluations and so give everyone higher ratings (leniency bias), while other research shows that ratings tend to be toward the average as evaluators find it difficult to differentiate between people (centrality bias).[26] Some evaluators also rate their employees higher because this also reflects on their performance and how they are as a manager (self-serving bias).

How to Improve Subjective Evaluations?

The growing popularity of subjective evaluations and the problems associated with poor subjective evaluations warrant attention. One of the ways to improve subjective evaluations is to train the evaluators in the process of evaluation. The process of setting up the objectives or goals of the manager at the start of the year must be clearly followed. Subordinates need to receive regular feedback on their performance. They are able to make the changes necessary to meet their targets. In addition, the evaluation processes should follow the elements of natural justice: ensuring fair processes where the subordinates are able to voice their opinions, treating all subordinates fairly and equally, and ensuring the evaluation procedures are laid out well in advance and adhered to.[27] These issues are all important in ensuring managers can see the relationship between their actions, the target and rewards, the concept of line of sight we discuss in chapter 1.

Another point is to only use senior managers who have experience in the business unit. The evaluators have walked in that manager's shoes for that business unit, recognizing the limitations in performance measures, and taking into account other factors. If target setting is an *art*, then the subjective use of a range of targets is the *art of arts*. Chapter 6 further develops the complexities with using multiple targets for financial and nonfinancial measures.

Summary

Change is inevitable. Target setting is based on certain conditions. When subsequent conditions change, the targets need to be reviewed. In the budgeting process, fixed targets and standard costs are useful for organizations operating in stable environments. Variance analysis is one way to update the fixed budget targets. When organizations are operating in dynamic environments, comparisons between actual performance and fixed budget targets result in poor decision making.

Targets can be made more flexible by adjusting the fixed budget numbers for the impact of changes in volumes and other factors. Rolling forecasts are another option where performances to targets for a few critical KPIs (financial and nonfinancial) are regularly updated so they indicate the expected level of performance. Relative performance targets can also be used to make performance targets more flexible.

Taking a more flexible and subjective approach to performance evaluation is growing in popularity, especially in incentive compensation contracts for senior managers. Traditionally, performance evaluations have been dominated by an objective approach whereby performance to quantitative targets (and usually financial targets) are evaluated based on preagreed standards. There are a number of problems with using objective performance to target comparisons (e.g., gaming, controllability issues). Using subjective performance evaluations allows superiors to adjust for differences between actual performance and the preset target by taking into account the uncontrollable, balancing short-term and long-term objectives, as well as the intangibles such as customer and employee relationships. Yet as the winds of change come through all forms of target setting, the realization is that only at the end of the day, with 20/20 hindsight, can you know with certainty what the business performance is or should have been. Target setting relies on the ability to look to the future, given the winds of uncertainty that blow your way as you stretch back the bow to take aim.

Key Learning Points

- Fixed budget targets are useful in organizations operating in stable environments.
- Variance analysis updates the fixed budget targets with current performance so that problems can be identified and corrected.
- Flexible budgeting involves understanding the cost-volume-profit relationships by restating the budget for key drivers such as sales volume.
- Rolling forecasts for critical KPIs are continually reviewed so they are good indications of the expected levels of performance.
- Financial and quantitative target comparisons are seen as more objective, but the measures are imperfect or incomplete, there are controllability issues, and there is often game playing associated with meeting the preset objective targets.
- Subjective uses of performance to target comparisons provide more flexibility in the evaluations because they take into account controllability issues, short-versus long-term strategic initiatives, and intangible benefits, but they can be seen as unfair and biased.

CHAPTER 4

Performance Targets

If you know the enemy and know yourself, you need not fear the result of a hundred battles.

—Sun Tzu, *The Art of War*

Introduction

The legendary quote of Sun Tzu highlights not only knowing oneself (the internal strengths and standards of excellence) but also knowing the enemy (the competitors' strengths and standards which they achieve). In this chapter we illustrate the importance of the different ways that targets can be set including: internal versus external targets, top-down versus bottom-up participation, negotiated targets, and ratcheting. Then we examine how forecasts and zero-based targets can be used to provide inputs into the target-setting process. Forecasts are what you expect to happen and sensitivity analysis can provide insights into the risks associated with the forecasts. Another approach is zero-based performance targets used to avoid being caught up with the past by looking to the future as a clean sheet of paper.

Don, a senior manager of a business unit, is about to set performance targets for one of his junior managers. He considers using relative performance targets but recognizes that it can be difficult to get comparable external and internal benchmarks. Another option is to negotiate with his junior manager, but he realizes that this can involve game playing. Maybe he should just use what the subordinate has achieved in the past and increase it to provide some stretch? Alternatively, he could ignore history and consider what type of performance targets the subordinate should be achieving. At the end of the day, should he just impose a target? We explore the process of setting performance targets first by looking at internal targets (what have you have done before) compared to external targets (what others do or expect to do).

Internal Versus External Targets

External targets are used when the performance being evaluated needs to be compared with what others do. Use internal targets when a business has unique competencies. External targets are often preferred as they are more objective. After all, managers are able to influence internal standards more than external standards.[1] External targets are based on competitor analysis or industry benchmarks that are indicative of best practices to which the business should strive. In other words, be as strong as your competitors in the war of winning the customer. One consequence of using internal standards for incentive compensation is that there is less variability in managers' incentive payments. The reason is that managers held to an internal standard are more likely to *manage* their earnings targets than those managers in organizations using external standards.[2] Managers can influence internally generated targets through income smoothing, building excessive slack, and other forms of game playing.

External Benchmarking

External standards are seen as more valid and objective than internal standards. The use of relative performance targets, benchmarks, and league tables shows great promise for performance management. The benefits from the process of benchmarking come from the sharing of information and ideas, working together, learning from other people, and improving processes. External benchmarks have value because competitors or the rest of your industry could be using these standards, and your business units need to deliver the same level of performance.

While externally generated targets have the potential to overcome many of the dysfunctional consequences of using internally generated standards, some evidence shows that they are not commonly used in incentive compensation plans.[3] The three main types of external benchmarking feature a range of advantages and disadvantages:[4]

- *Compared with competitors.* Benchmarking against direct competitors who have similar products or services is much better than using internal standards. The problem is that competitor data are rarely publicly available because of commercial sensitivity. It may also be a poor strategy to benchmark against competitors, rather than create a point of difference where your product sets the market, like Apple has done with the iPhone.

- *Functional or industry benchmarking.* This is where you benchmark yourself against competitors who have similar features in terms of operations, markets, and services. The lack of direct competition means that information is more likely to be shared. The downside is that these businesses are not direct competitors, and it can be less beneficial as the learning from other organizations may not result in large increases in improvement in key areas of the business.
- *Process or generic benchmarking.* This involves developing benchmarks by comparison with dissimilar organizations that have innovative processes for similar areas (e.g., distribution, logistics, supplier management).

Case Capsule 4.1 shows that using external benchmarks presents some problems in practice.

Some other disadvantages with external benchmarking include

- *The "not invented here" syndrome.* This occurs when there is resistance to adopting practices from elsewhere. We know of one organization with a processing unit that had won a Baldridge Award for Performance Excellence. Surprisingly, only managers from one of the many other processing sites within the organization came to see what the award-winning unit was doing. Clearly, if a best practice is outside a business unit or responsibility center, managers may be reluctant to accept and implement this best practice or external benchmark.
- *Data availability.* Collecting the data needed for benchmarking can also lead to problems. It is difficult to find two businesses or functional areas that are directly comparable. You need to understand the data, where it comes from, and what it includes. If you are comparing *apples* with *oranges*, it can take a lot of effort to rework the data to make it directly comparable. On the other hand, if you do not make it comparable then this leads to arguments between managers that their organization

Case Capsule 4.1. Benchmarking in Hospitals

One study of hospitals in the United Kingdom has examined the use of relative performance evaluation to benchmark hospital costs and to create a league table (the "ladder of success").[5] Benchmarking had the potential to provide information to hospitals on how they were performing compared with other hospitals and to help them work toward achieving best in the industry. However, implementing this has not been easy. The findings show that rather than providing benchmarks for performance excellence, the benchmarking process encouraged the focus on average costs. Major problems were caused because of the poor data quality, and this may explain why there were significant jumps and falls in the hospital rankings each year. Another issue is that the focus on cost does not consider other key performance variables such as quality or service. They also had problems because of the lack of standardization of the data and because of the differences in the hospitals being compared. The focus has been on highlighting the top performers and shaming the poor performers, rather than focusing on improving processes and learning outcomes.

cannot be benchmarked against competitors for a number of reasons. In large organizations, often high support costs need to be charged to the business units. This leads to arguments that the internal overhead costs are higher than their competitors pay, such as for property costs, repairs and maintenance, information technology costs, and treasury services to administer foreign currency fluctuations.

- *Not for differentiated services.* Benchmarking is useful for standardized services and where comparisons of costs and services are comparable across business units in the same industry. Benchmarks are not useful when you want to differentiate your services. Robert Kaplan says that differentiating support services, which focus on providing solutions to internal customers and being trusted partners and advisers to the internal business units, is a better option.[6] Such a co-creation of value is often difficult with third parties. Therefore, by using external benchmarking you could lose sight of what makes your business excellent and you could end up copying the competition. To differentiate key services, our recommendation would be for internal benchmarking, where your business's unique view on servicing customer expectations can be enhanced. In other words, ask your customers what the standards should be. Do not base your standards on the competitors when you are different.

Internal Benchmarking

Internal benchmarking requires organizations to identify parts of the business that have similar processes and then identify the best processes. The advantages include the communication and information sharing between various parts of the business. The disadvantages with internal standards are that they can only highlight the improvement over time and do not provide any evidence that the level of performance is industry best practice or meets customers' expectations.

If you use internal benchmarking, you need to coordinate the views of managers whose operations rely on each other to understand what type of performance is needed for excellence. Take centralized information technology (IT) services as an example. The traditional way is to focus on a cost per unit and then to drive down the cost. However, it is likely to be nonfinancial targets such as range of services, timeliness of response, or cocreation of value, which are held by the intermediate customers to be important.

In some cases it is important to focus on protecting uniqueness. It can be detrimental to an organization to import best practices into IT services and then require marketing, production, and logistics to change without recognizing their special needs. In a brewery, for example, the need to change the IT support arose from the need to upgrade software. While the software giant chosen to provide the upgrade had other breweries and the best practices mapped out, this brewery decided to keep what was its strategic advantage in-house. The brewery wanted to protect its specialty beers, which targeted three geographic zones and specific customer preferences. The IT support center customized the software incrementally, phasing in the implementation to suit production and marketing managers' needs and expectations. The targets for the introduction of the

IT services were set around meeting the financial, nonfinancial, operating, and strategic data needs of the marketing, production, and logistics units. As the new software was incrementally implemented, the IT support services had not merely to understand the short-term needs of the intermediate customers (marketing, production, and logistics) but also to forecast the medium- and long-term needs to ensure that the niche brewing market, the unique distribution channels, as well as the end-customer needs were being met. The role of forecasts by the intermediate customers became pivotal to this success story of a centralized shared resource, the IT support department.

Having decided if internal or external benchmarking is going to form the basis of target setting, the notion of relative performance evaluation needs to be understood.

Relative Performance Targets

Relative performance evaluation is a comparison of the business performance using internal or external benchmarks. Relative performance evaluation implies that common measures must be used, but most organizations try and differentiate themselves and so it is their customized measures that are most important. This also means it is difficult to find external units that can be used for comparison.[7] Relative performance evaluation systems can also result in gaming, as managers in the peer organizations could work together to lower the performance bar for everyone.

A study of a relative performance contract at the Korean Post Office highlights how it is critical to establish targets that employees perceive are fair, and to take into account the differences between the stores when putting them into reference groups (see Case Capsule 4.2).[8]

While targets can be used in relative performance evaluation, understanding the impact of top-down or bottom-up participation, and negotiation needs to be considered.

Target-Setting Strategies

Three other approaches businesses use to set targets include: top-down target setting, bottom-up participation and negotiation. Each of these inputs to target setting highlight the influence different people have in

Case Capsule 4.2. The Korean Post Office

The Korean Post Office sought to implement relative performance evaluations by benchmarking and evaluating stores compared to their peers.[9] To do this the stores were put into nine benchmark groups along with other stores that operated in similar environments (e.g., stores in Seoul, regional stores). The performance measures were store profitability (e.g., store revenues divided by store operating cost) and productivity (e.g., mail volumes handled per store employee, divided by the average productivity in the reference group). The results show that the new relative performance evaluation system did improve financial performance at the store level, except in those stores who felt the new system was unfair. The perceptions of unfairness may have arisen from the competition between unit managers as bonuses were only available for those who performed in the top 50% of the peer group. Another cause of the perceived unfairness is the comparison of apples to oranges. Determining the reference groups was difficult as the stores differed on a range of factors including geographic location, customer needs, volume, and competition. For example, it would be unfair to compare a rural post office against a metropolitan post office. To map best practices of a metropolitan post office and implement these processes at a rural post office, the latter having different customer needs, can indeed be detrimental to the customers in that rural region. The case highlights that fairness in performance evaluation is important, especially the factors managers had little control over, and understanding the customer base at different stores is central to relative performance evaluation.

setting the targets. The level of influence employees have in setting performance targets influences their motivation, commitment to achieving the targets, and willingness to share information.

Top-Down Target Setting

A top-down approach to target setting means that senior management sets the target levels to be achieved. The main advantage of a top-down approach in budgeting is that it allows senior management to set the level of target difficulty. This avoids any game playing and time-consuming negotiations associated with allowing lower-level employees to participate in setting targets. The disadvantages with imposed targets are that they can be seen as unfair and unachievable and so are unlikely to encourage subordinates to commit to meeting the targets. Top-down targets also mean that the lower-level managers have little understanding of the assumptions and the calculations behind the targets.

Top-down targets are only appropriate in certain circumstances. For example, where targets can be set using engineered standards or historical trends, or where relative performance measures are available. Top-down targets are also appropriate when senior managers have a good understanding of the business because they have come up through the ranks, or where subordinates are inexperienced at budgeting.[10]

The opposite of the top-down approach is to allow people to participate in setting targets.

Bottom-Up Participation

It is intuitive that participation in setting targets leads to better performance. This also seems to be the trend in practice. A recent survey examining budgeting practices in the United States and Canada suggests that companies are changing their budgeting systems to incorporate information from frontline managers and to take a more bottom-up approach.[11] Let us look at some of the benefits of participation in target setting.

Encouraging people to participate in setting targets can lead to greater commitment to achieve the targets, as people are more likely to take ownership and make the required changes. Another reason is it improves communication across the various areas in an organization. For example, lower-level managers can provide information to senior managers on strategic opportunities, and top-level managers can ensure the organizational vision and priorities are clear down the levels.

Participation also allows people to use their knowledge and experience to improve decision making. This can help clarify what is expected, and people become more aware of what they can do to meet the targets. For example, managers can assess the operating environment, and this improves their understanding of the various alternatives to meet the targets.

Participation in budgets has also been argued to reduce stress, and this reduces the dysfunctional consequences such as game playing.[12] A person's motivation can be influenced by the amount of financial risk imposed on him or her. For example, if a person's incentive compensation depends on a comparison between actual production cost and the cost budget, the financial risk to the manager will vary if his cost budget is fixed or flexible (as discussed in chapter 3). Therefore, the use of the appropriate profit target based on the type of budget (fixed or flexible) can influence both motivation and risk. Another aspect of risk sharing is participation. If an employer wishes their subordinates to share in the risk, sharing information as well as participating in the target-setting process is important.

However, participation in budgeting does have its downsides. Managers may seek to achieve their personal goals as well as the firm goals by negotiating easy targets (often called slack or padding).[13] Slack is the difference between the resources stated in the budget and the actual resources needed to do the job. For example, an employee may state that it takes an hour to machine a part, knowing that it will take him only 40 minutes. This difference of 20 minutes between the stated time (budgeted time) and the actual time is *slack*. Excessive slack is a problem because this means that resources have been allocated to the wrong areas.

Giving managers some slack does have advantages. For example, slack provides managers with some flexibility in operations and allows them to take some strategic actions without having to get approval for resources to make small changes.

Negotiating Budget Targets

Negotiation is common in setting profit or investment center budget targets because the senior managers have more knowledge about the organizational objectives and resource issues, whereas the business unit managers have more information on what the unit can achieve given their opportunities and constraints. This imbalance in information is called *information asymmetry* in agency theory.[14] The negotiation process means that the two groups (senior managers and business unit managers) have to share some information with each other.

The result of the negotiations can be affected by the relative political power of the parties (e.g., small versus large business units) and the negotiating skills of the senior managers and the lower-level managers. The negotiation process can also result in gaming. For example, the business unit managers can take advantage of their superior knowledge about what targets the business unit could achieve and negotiate lower targets with senior management. We know of one business unit manager who subsequently set much higher targets internally for the people in the business unit to achieve, resulting in very high short-term profits.

The level that budget targets are negotiated can have important implications. The managers who are negotiating targets for their business units are highly aware of the fact that, if they agree to targets that are too difficult to achieve, they will have demotivated their whole team, especially if there are financial consequences from not meeting or exceeding the targets. If the targets are too easy, this can make it difficult for the managers to motivate their subordinates. The managers may also damage their reputation in the organization if they try to negotiate targets that are perceived as being too easy. At the other extreme, if senior managers let the business units agree to unrealistic targets, this can result in not achieving the overall organizational performance targets.

In contrast to negotiating targets, sometimes senior managers impose targets and continually increase the targets each year. Or, as the saying goes: "Keep tightening the belt until someone squeals, then you know it is as tight as it can go." This saying probably sums up some senior managers' views on ratcheting—keep tightening the belt until there is real pain.

Ratcheting

Ratcheting is where last year's numbers are tightened or ratcheted up year after year. In relation to health and safety measures, achieving a target such as a 10% decrease in accidents one year would be followed by a further 10% decrease in the targets the next year, and so on. The purpose of ratcheting performance targets is to put pressure on managers to continually improve performance. Figure 4.1 illustrates ratcheting.

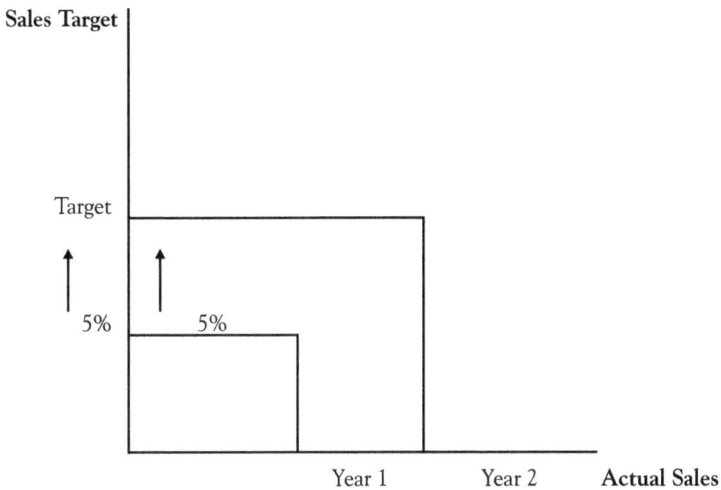

Figure 4.1. Ratcheting.

Ratcheting can cause managers to play a number of games to avoid being held to higher targets in the future. This includes focusing managers' attention on just meeting the budget target, or, in a good year, moving some sales to the future period, or making accounting adjustments to decrease earnings.[15] Another example is that ratcheting can push managers to work hard, but only every other year![16]

Ratcheting can also encourage managers to delay some strategic initiatives or at least spread their implementation over a number of years.[17] The problem for managers is that if they include strategic initiatives such as new products or process improvements in the current targets, then this higher level of performance is *expected*. Managers feel they are not being rewarded for the increased performance because the benefits of the strategic initiatives are already factored into the budget.

The level of ratcheting may be different depending on whether the prior financial performance was a profit or a loss.[18] Research has found that managers in well-performing businesses are also more likely to exceed their targets, compared with those operating in loss-making businesses.[19]

To overcome the ratcheting problem in budgeting, targets may be developed through forecasting or using zero-based targets. These approaches can be inputs into the target setting process.

Forecasts

If you don't know where you are going, you might wind up someplace else.

—Yogi Berra

Forecasts are a statement of what you think will happen, and the purpose of forecasts is to support decision making and help create the future.[20] To know where you are going is pivotal as you could get lost, as Yogi Berra noted.

The accuracy of forecasts may determine the way in which targets are set. For example, accurate forecasts may lead directly to top-down targets. However, when environmental factors (e.g., changing customer demands, complex supplier chain relationships, to name a few) reduce the accuracy of forecasts, a more participatory approach is needed. Under such changing factors, participation by lower-level managers can result in greater confidence in estimating probabilities, as well as gaining commitment from managers to achieve the negotiated targets in the face of volatile conditions. It is also best to ensure that the people doing the forecasting are not isolated from the operational levels, as this can result in poor communication and understanding of the budget.[21] Forecasts are an integral part of the budgeting process.

When developing forecasts for budgets you need to predict the future and make some assumptions about what is likely to happen. This is always difficult. One of the first steps in creating the budget is developing assumptions about the following:

- What is going to happen in the economy?
- What level of sales is likely?
- What is the likely price of key inputs such as wages, petrol, diesel, and so on?

One of the problems with traditional budgeting has been that the assumptions underlying the budgets are often implicit rather than explicit or are developed with little analysis.[22] Research by the Hackett Group of more than 70 large U.S. and European companies finds that two-thirds of organizations miss their quarterly earnings forecasts by between 6% and 30%, and more than half the companies could not accurately forecast sales for the next quarter.[23] The Hackett Group argues that fore-casting is becoming more difficult for organizations because of high risk and volatility. The ways they recommend to improve forecasting include the following:

- using rolling forecasts;
- evaluating risk and volatility;
- reviewing forecast accuracy to learn from prior experiences.

Assessing the risk that the forecasts will not be achieved is an important part of forecasting. One case study found that risk had been considered by managers in the budgeting process of four organizations, but the risk analysis was not evident in the budget documents that included just single-point estimates.[24] There was also little evidence of risk modeling in the four cases. This may be because the forecasting was done right at the beginning, and then once the average or expected levels were achieved, they were not included in the budget documents. Organizations may include statements of the risks in achieving the budget targets, but this could be in the discussion, rather than in the final budget document.

There are a number of ways to make forecasts. The simplest way is to input all the key drivers into the budget to estimate net profit. While this is simple, it does not tell you anything about the chance of achieving this level of financial performance or how to improve the performance by managing certain key resources. To understand the effect of key drivers on the budget, you can use a range of tools and techniques such as sensitivity analysis, probability analysis, and decision trees. Sensitivity analysis is discussed next, and an example of probability analysis is given in the appendix.

Sensitivity Analysis

Sensitivity analysis, when used in budgeting, is an important tool as it shows us how sensitive the budget is to changes in key drivers of the business. This type of analysis is commonly used to provide information for setting performance targets for budgets, for key performance indicators (KPIs), and for strategic projects. The first step in scenario analysis (also called *what if* analysis) is to identify the key drivers of the business, and then to examine the effect changes in these key drivers have on the budget. The key drivers also highlight the areas most at risk.

Different scenarios are developed to see the impact of various changes on the budget. For example, what if sales increased by 5%, 10%, or 20%? What is the impact of these various scenarios on the final budget figure? What if there is a major shock to the economy that we did not expect? The information provided for these questions can be critical as it shows the potential impact on the budget target if your assumptions are wrong.

Table 4.1 illustrates how you can look at historical data and then use this to analyze the effect on the budget from what is expected (the base or average case), the best case scenario, and the worst case scenario. If the best level of sales is $600,000, the expected level is $500,000, and the worst level is $525,000, we can use probabilities to estimate what is highly likely to be the actual sales ($505,000 as shown in Table 4.1). This analysis is easily done using spreadsheets or accounting software.

Sensitivity analysis shows the extent to which budgets (e.g., sales budgets) are affected by some key drivers, whereas forecasting can be used to understand more about the probability that the budget target will be achieved. For planning purposes, it is more important to know the probability distribution of the budget, rather than a single point estimate. Once a draft of the budget has been prepared, then it is possible to substitute probability estimates for each of the key drivers.[25]

If you are interested in knowing more about probability analysis, we provide a practical example in the appendix at the end of this book that analyzes the probability of achieving sales targets.

Another approach to target setting is to ignore what has happened in the past and start afresh.

Table 4.1. Scenario Analysis

	Best case	**Expected case**	**Worst case**	
Increase	20%	10%	5%	
Sales	600,000	500,000	525,000	
Probability	0.1	0.7	0.2	
Expected	60,000	350,000	105,000	505,000

Zero-Based Performance Targets

A zero-based approach starts with the basic question: What is needed right now without being constrained by the past? It is like starting with a blank sheet of paper and determining what is best or needed. For example, with regard to health and safety, if the target is to be in the top 25% of companies in your industry, you then look at all aspects of health and safety in your business, without being constrained by the past.

Therefore, zero-based performance targets can use external standards, forecasts of what the market can accept, or develop internal standards that exceed competitors. A caution in zero-based performance targets is not to throw out your unique competencies and business processes in which you excel.

A zero-based budgeting approach can be undertaken in various ways. One approach is to develop targets for revenues and costs as if setting up a new business, that is, without referring back to prior years. The argument is that just because certain costs were covered in the past this is no justification for including them in the budget. A weaker form of this approach is to critically evaluate each item in the budget and include a review process.[26] While zero-based budgeting is supposed to overcome many of the problems with traditional budgets based on prior performance, they are seldom used.[27] The main reasons for this are the time and cost involved, and problems with data gathering. This approach could be valuable if used as a one-off exercise when there was substantial change, but there would be little advantage for organizations operating in a stable environment to do this each year.[28]

Summary

Sun Tzu's quote at the start of this chapter sums up what a business needs to do. Know your internal strengths and weaknesses as well as what the competitors do better than you. This requires an appreciation of internal and external benchmarks, which highlight the battleground ahead.

There are growing calls for new and innovative ways to set performance targets. External targets are used when comparisons to competitors is important, and are seen as more objective. Internal targets are used when uniqueness is important or when external targets are not available.

Relative performance targets and external targets are less able to be manipulated than internal targets. However, it is important the targets are perceived as fair and the reference groups for comparison purposes are carefully selected.

The easiest way for top managers is to impose the targets on the subordinates, but this is rarely appropriate. In most situations, top-down targets result in the perception that the targets are unachievable and unfair, and thus they do not encourage commitment to the targets. Encouraging participation by lower-level managers is becoming more common because of the many benefits, including commitment to achieving the targets, improved decision making, and reduced tension and stress. Negotiated targets are often used at the business unit level because top managers have less information on the capabilities of the business unit than the managers. The problems here are that the negotiations are affected by politics, negotiating skills, and gaming. Ratcheting bases targets on past performance and these targets are continually increased each year to place pressure on managers.

Forecasts can be useful inputs to developing targets. It is important to know where you are going and to be aware of the risks associated with key drivers of the forecasts. Some techniques such as sensitivity analysis and probability analysis can assist with forecasting. If you wish to start from scratch, then zero-based targets can be used.

Key Learning Points

- External targets focusing on best-in-class benchmarks are more objective and less able to be influenced by managers, but good comparative data can be difficult to obtain.
- Internal targets are useful when it is important to be unique and to differentiate yourself from competitors. The problem is that this may not lead to industry best practice.
- Top-down, imposed targets are used where standards are available to set targets (e.g., engineered costs). However, top-down targets are often seen as unachievable and unfair.
- Encouraging participation in target setting can improve managers' commitment and motivation, improve decision making,

and reduce stress and tension. However, it can lead to easier targets and building excessive slack.

- Negotiated targets are common at the business unit level because of the imbalance of information between the units and top management.
- Ratcheted targets are based solely on history, do not take into account changing conditions, and can influence managers to play games such as smoothing income and working hard every second year.
- Forecasts are estimates of what you expect to happen and they can be useful inputs into the target-setting process. Sensitivity analysis and risk analysis are important techniques to assist in developing forecasts.
- Zero-based targets ignore past history and establish targets as if they were for a new business.

CHAPTER 5

Target Difficulty

When you aim for perfection, you discover it's a moving target.

—George Fisher

Introduction

Determining how difficult targets should be is one of the critical choices to be made in target setting.[1] Should targets be set at a very challenging level? Olympian targets that only the top performers could be expected to achieve? That is the pursuit of excellence. Yet many will fail in the Olympics. Similarly, Olympian targets demotivate all but the top performing managers. Or should targets be set at a level that is likely to be achieved? If targets are highly achievable how do you motivate managers to increase performance beyond the target? The *art* of target setting is to chose the right level of target difficulty for the business unit and the manager. The challenge is the targets, once set, should not remain static, as organizations operate in a continually-changing environment, such as shifting competitor positions and changing customer expectations. Rather, the organization learns and adapts to the changing forces and, therefore, so should the targets.

Traditionally one budget target is used for conflicting purposes, such as motivation, planning, and coordination, as discussed in chapter 2. Or should you use different targets for different purposes? A stretch sales target used to motivate employees needs to have some degree of difficulty, whereas the forecasted level of sales needed for planning and coordination purposes needs to be what is expected to be achieved. In this chapter we draw on lessons learnt from setting budget targets to provide insights into setting targets for other financial and nonfinancial measures.

How Difficult Should Motivational Targets Be?

There is debate in the literature as to how challenging performance targets should be set to motivate managers to increase performance. Goal-setting theory finds that setting targets is more motivating than asking people to *do their best*.[2] If the targets are too easy, then people are unlikely to try and perform better once they have met the target. We use the term *stretch* target to indicate that the target has been set above what would normally be expected.[3] Stretch targets can be powerful motivators, so long as they are not perceived by employees as being so difficult that they are unachievable and the targets are worth reaching.[4] Target setting can be described as more of an *art than a science* as it is often difficult to determine how easy or difficult the targets have been set, without the benefit of hindsight.[5]

To understand how to set motivational targets we examine why targets are useful to motivate better performance, the problems with using Olympian targets, highly achievable targets, and the use of capped performance targets.

Goal-Setting Theory

Do targets motivate people to increase their performance? Insights into this question come from goal-setting theory, which has been developed over a 30-year period by Locke and Latham. The goal-setting studies show that clear stretch performance targets lead to higher performance than vague goals such as *do your best*.[6] The goal-setting studies also show that so long as employees are committed to the targets, have the ability to achieve the targets, and do not have conflicts between competing targets, higher target difficulty leads to higher performance.

In one study, truck drivers were encouraged to increase the weight of each of their truck loads. Two groups of truck drivers were either told to do their best or work toward preset difficult targets.[7] The truck drivers who were set difficult targets and paid a per-piece rate performed better than drivers who were told to do their best. One of the reasons for this was that the employees knew what they were expected to do.[8] This simple focused target (e.g., loading the trucks to the maximum legal weight) allowed the employees to understand what was required to do the job by reducing ambiguity and may have also reduced their feelings of being overwhelmed. A learning effect resulted because the truck drivers made modifications to their trucks so that they could improve their understanding of the load weights before driving to the weighting station.[9]

Clear and specific performance targets enhance employees' line of sight. Targets are more motivating where employees have clear line of sight between their actions, performance, and rewards (see chapter 1). When people are committed to achieving the target, they need to receive feedback on their progress toward the target so know their current performance and have the opportunity to think of ways to improve their performance. Where the tasks are complex, people can become motivated to use their talents to work out new ways to achieve the results.[10]

Goal-setting theory draws upon Taylor's *Principles of Scientific Management*.[11] Activities and processes are broken down into components, which are further simplified. Employees doing these specialized tasks are advised how to undertake their work, including the duration of breaks, to increase productivity. This extract from Taylor's study describes the target setting process for employees carrying steel at Bethlehem Steel Mill:

> The best way to do this is to . . . divide the man's work into its elements and time each element separately. For example, in the case of a man loading pig-iron on to a car, the elements should be (a) picking up the pig from the ground or pile (time in hundredths of a minute); (b) walking with it on a level (time per foot walked) . . . Two elements important to the success of this work should be noted: *First*, on the morning following each day's work, each workman was given a slip of paper informing him in detail of just how much work he had done the day before, and the amount he had earned. This enabled him to measure his performance against his earnings while the details were fresh in his mind . . . *Second*, each man's work was measured by itself. Only when absolutely necessary was the work of two men measured up together and the price divided between them, and care was taken to select two men of as nearly as possible the same capacity.[12]

Taylor's whole system rests on accurate performance measures, regular and timely feedback, and clearly identifying individual performance rather than team performance. The challenge is to draw insights from the goal-setting studies to provide practical advice for managers in complex settings like organizations.[13] Managers often have to rely on the work of others to meet their targets, the tasks are complex, and the financial and nonfinancial performance measures used are often incomplete or inaccurate. For example, the conditions may change (e.g., the global financial crisis) and the preset level of the target can become be too difficult (i.e. Olympian). Under these conditions, employees should learn how to cope with the present and plan for the future rather than being blamed for not meeting past targets. In other situations where tasks are complex the aim is to acquire new skills. This requires learning targets, rather than performance targets.[14]

Goal-setting theory has been the subject of recent debate. A narrow focus on goals can generate dysfunctional behaviors, such as risk taking by managers and employees, gaming and unethical behavior, decreasing intrinsic motivation, reducing cooperation between business units, and an inhibition of learning.[15] Difficult goals can reduce employee commitment to the goals.[16] Targets imposed by top management with little participation from key employees can also lead to temptation for gaming, arguments over the controllability of the outcomes and unethical behavior (as discussed in chapter 4).

Olympian Targets

Olympian targets are where the level of difficulty is set so high that only excellent athletes, brilliant managers and only the top employees can achieve them. These top performers will work their best to achieve these targets, and this can result in incredible gains in productivity, sales, improved cash flows, and profitability. While these Olympian targets sound great, there is a downside. If these Olympian targets are used for performance evaluations and not achieving these targets is viewed as failure, there can be serious consequences.[17] Employees see themselves as failures, managers could lose control as burnout takes hold on employees, and cooperation between people across the organization fails.[18] Therefore, Olympian targets used for motivational purposes can result in high levels of job-related stress, game playing, and fraud.

Excessive tension can be an insidious force that frustrates a manager and ultimately leads to reduced performance from physical exhaustion and mental fatigue. Managers tend to become frustrated, apathetic, and slow to make decisions and will adopt various coping mechanisms in an attempt to relieve stress. One study reports managers experiencing job-related tension have reduced respect and trust for their superiors.[19] This prevented the exchange of information about job-related difficulties and problems, resulting in lack of cooperation and coordination of essential activities. Increased data manipulation and the gaming of performance indicators, inherent in budget gamesmanship, is the result. Other coping behaviors include alienation, employee absenteeism and turnover, social withdrawal, decreased altruism, and escapist drinking. Therefore, excessive job-related tension arising from unachievable targets needs to be avoided.

Stress and tension around the level of target difficulty can impact on performance. The Yerkes-Dodson Law argues that there is an inverted-U relationship between stressors, such as target difficulty and performance.[20] The argument is that performance increases with rising difficulty, but only up to a certain point, and then increasing difficulty can cause a decrease in performance.[21] Figure 5.1 shows the relationship between target difficulty (e.g., stress) and performance. Up to a certain level, the higher the target difficulty, the higher the performance, but only up to the point where targets are still perceived as achievable. Targets that are seen as unachievable are not motivating, and performance decreases. The *art* of target setting is to know where the turning point is!

Setting Olympian targets can have serious consequences for organizations, such as gaming and other dysfunctional behaviors. Let us return to the Sears, Roebuck and Co. example from chapter 1. Setting very difficult targets resulted in employees taking a number of actions such as overcharging for work and carrying out unnecessary repairs to meet the targets.

A recent survey of budgeting practices in the United States and Canada has shown that gaming budget targets is a problem in both countries.[22] Managers admitted that in the prior two years these actions were taken in their business units: deferring necessary expenditure (91% U.S., 80% Canada), negotiating easier targets (86% U.S., 77% Canada), bringing forward expenditures when a target is not attainable (taking a "big bath"; 70% U.S., 47% Canada), accelerating sales near year end to

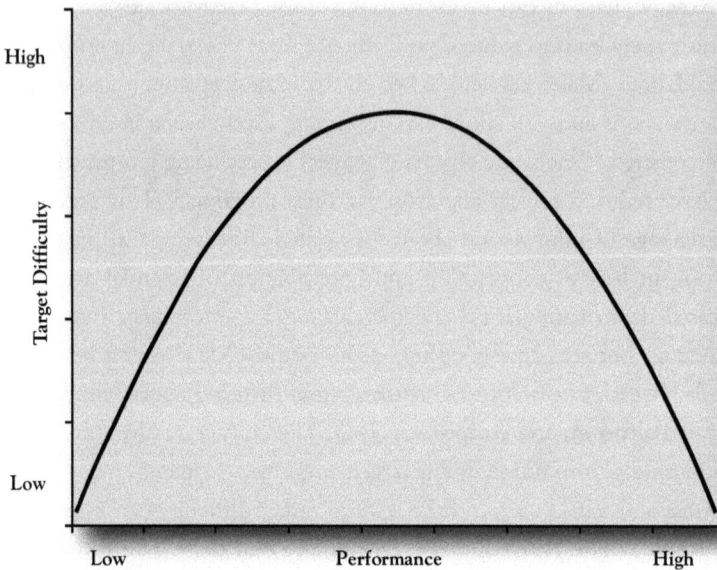

Figure 5.1. Target difficulty versus performance.

make the budget (61% U.S., 44% Canada), and spending money at the end of the year to avoid losing it (80% U.S., 42% Canada).

Highly Achievable Targets

The traditional view on target setting was that the more difficult the target, the more motivating it would be because it would push employees to be more innovative and to achieve higher performance than if easier targets were set.[23] This was until Merchant and Manzoni's study found that in most organizations the budget targets appeared to be set at levels where there was a high expectation that the targets would be achieved.[24] Highly achievable targets are not easy targets, but budget targets that are achievable 80–90% of the time by a hard-working manager. The *art* is to know the level to set targets without the benefit of hindsight. Targets set by managers and their superiors have a high probability of achievement because they[25]

- increase managers' *commitment* to the targets;
- create a *winning* culture by increasing managers' confidence in their ability to reach subsequent targets;

- *lower control costs*. When performance targets are likely to be closer to target (e.g., budget), there is less monitoring, exception reporting, and the need to explain the variances;
- encourage *less gaming* of the financial information to meet the targets. With difficult targets, managers have strong incentives to manipulate the data to reach the targets;
- give greater *operating flexibility* and flexibility to build in some *slack* so that effective managers can think more creatively or quickly adapt to changing circumstances;
- protect against *overoptimistic* budget forecasts from managers. This means that top management has more confidence that the budget targets will be achieved for the organization;
- ensure that remuneration packages are *competitive* by linking targets to bonuses.

To ensure the highly achievable targets remain motivational, organizations often use capped performance targets linked to rewards.

Capped Targets Used for Incentive Compensation

The purpose of using capped targets is to motivate managers to keep trying to improve performance whether they are below or above the expected performance target. Figure 5.2 shows a typical incentive compensation system that sets a hurdle rate below which no bonuses are paid (point A, called a threshold).[26] The minimum is the amount paid when the threshold is reached and incentives are being paid (point B). The performance target is located somewhere along the payout line between the minimum and maximum levels (point C). The target level is generally expected to be achieved by managers.[27] The maximum is the cutoff point when no bonuses are to be paid (point D). The following diagram also illustrates the relationship between target difficulty (higher performance) and managers' incentive compensation.

The slope of the line between points B and D can be linear, convex, or concave. Linear plans are when the slope is constant between the minimum, the target, and the maximum (see Figure 5.2). Concave plans are bowl shaped (see point E), whereas convex plans are the opposite (see point F).[28] One U.S. survey shows that 45% of the 20 companies that

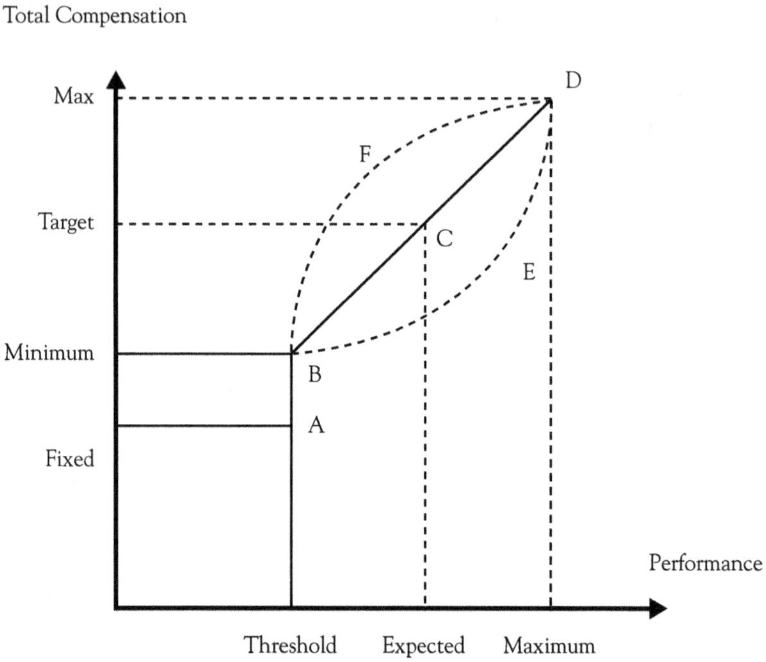

Total Compensation

Figure 5.2. Capped performance targets used for incentive compensation.

used external standards had linear payout lines, compared to 13% of the 135 companies that used internal standards.[29] The companies that used internal standards were more likely to use convex-shaped bonus plans (28%) than concave ones (20%). Managers have different incentives toward dysfunctional behavior depending on the type of payout line (e.g., linear, convex, concave).

The kinks in the pay-off line (at points B and D) also provide opportunities for managers to engage in dysfunctional behaviors to meet the performance targets.[30] Put yourself in the shoes of a manager being rewarded in this way. If you are going to have a bad year, then you may as well *take a bath* by making the loss as big as possible (e.g., by writing off provisions, delaying sales). The reason is to carry forward earnings into the next period to improve the bonus for the future year. In order to meet or exceed your current budget target, then it may be necessary to increase current profits (e.g., delaying expenditure, bring forward revenues). If it is a great year and you are going to exceed your maximum, then *go fishing or golfing!* The maximum cutoff provides incentives for managers to push profits over to the following year (e.g., paying expenses in advance, delaying revenues). These types of gaming behaviors are widespread.[31]

Despite the potential for gaming, organizations prefer to set upper limits for bonuses as they wish to avoid the publicity that arises when managers receive large bonus payments. A good example of this has been the bankers' bonuses in the United States, United Kingdom, and France that have received so much bad publicity. A second reason is that using capped performance targets reduces the risk to managers associated with missing their budget targets and increases the chance that they will at least get some bonus, especially when the target level is highly achievable. Other reasons include avoiding high bonuses from windfall gains, under the fear that it further encourages short-term gains at the expense of the longer term; ensuring lower managers do not receive more pay than senior managers; keeping bonuses consistent over time; and recognizing that the incentive compensation system design may be flawed, and this can protect the company from unforeseen consequences.[32]

How to Set the Spread Between Minimum-Target-Maximum

The target level is typically expected to be achieved (i.e., highly achievable).[33] The threshold targets are expected to be the minimum performance level at which any portion of a bonus is paid. The maximum targets are expected to be Olympian targets that are almost impossible to achieve. Usually the upper target limit is outside the business-as-usual range, and Walsh estimates the chance of achieving maximum as "statistically less than 15 in 1,000."[34]

There is little advice on how to set the spread between the minimum, the target, and the maximum. While the threshold level is generally easily reached, the spread between minimum and maximum may indicate a lack of precision in the performance measures, and managers' ability to control financial or nonfinancial measures.[35]

In one organization, we examined documents that show the executives use judgment and take into account the maturity of the business (e.g., mature or start-up); the degree of target difficulty, economic and competitor activity; and what they called the "need to perform."[36] In this organization their rough rule of thumb was that thresholds should be set at 80% of budget, and maximums should be set at 120% of budget. But the actual thresholds and maximums deviated from that rule of thumb because the risks and opportunities varied significantly across business units. The executives said that for business units operating in uncertain environments the threshold was set at 80% of budget, while in some stable business units, the threshold was set at 95% of budget. Similarly, judgment was involved in the setting of the performance maximums, which were intended to be very difficult targets involving considerable stretch. The performance targets, thresholds, and maximums were peer-reviewed by the entire senior management team.

So far we have focused on how difficult targets should be to motivate employees. Next, we focus on target difficulty for other purposes.

Should Different Targets Be Used for Different Purposes?

Targets are used for multiple purposes, so it makes sense that the level of target difficulty should depend on the purposes they are being used for. Organizations can use Olympian targets as directions or compass points to orient future operational, tactical, and strategic measures. Olympian targets can therefore be inspirational or provide a future vision. However, care needs to be taken if you use Olympian targets to also motivate managers. While motivational targets need some degree of stretch, once the targets are perceived as being unachievable, they become demotivating and can result in gaming behaviors.

Targets used for planning, forecasting, resource allocations, control, and coordination need to be set at levels that are *expected* to be achieved (see chapter 2). When targets are used for planning and coordination purposes, they help managers make a number of decisions: How many employees are needed? What level of inventory is required to meet the projected sales? How much cash is needed to ensure payments to employees and suppliers are made on time? There is little point in planning operations based on targets that are not likely to be achieved.[37] Similarly, expected levels of performance are important for control issues as this reduces the amount of monitoring and exception reporting.

A problem with the traditional budgeting approach is that one budget target is used for a range of conflicting purposes including motivation, planning, and control. An option is to use different targets for different purposes. For example, in times of economic downturns, spending is often reduced on discretionary strategic issues (e.g., research and development). The reason is that cutting these discretionary costs is often seen as a "magic bullet" to quickly improve short-term profits. The problem is that these cuts can have long-term consequences. When the recession passes, the market picks up, the company may suffer from a lack of employee training, market development, and research and development. Competitors gain market share and become the top of mind recall from the customer.

The following discussion highlights some of the problems when the targets used for budgetary control have negative effects on resource allocation for strategic issues (e.g., employee training, market development, research and development). You need to avoid using difficult budget targets for control as this can reduce resource allocation for strategic initiatives.

Why Protect Employee Training?

Most developed countries find it hard to keep abreast of the cheaper manufacturing sites in China, and the ASEAN (Association of Southeast Asian Nations) Tigers. As one hulking German glassblower stated with great pride, "I go for training 6 times a year so that when I create new glass art, I am ahead of the cheaper Bohemian glass makers." In this way, the German glassblower ensured that his products are different from the cheaper products manufactured in other parts of the world. Employee training targets (e.g., a percentage spent per dollar of revenue) empower employees to look at the technical aspects of their job and to be at the forefront of technology; they also add value in terms of service and product development. These attributes are hard to replicate or duplicate by competitors. Google is a good example of these types of innovative practices. Google employees are encouraged to spend 20% of their time on ideas for new projects. Training opportunities increase employee motivation and job satisfaction. A good idea is to map the competencies that employees need to implement the strategic initiatives and link them to training programs.

Why Protect Market Development?

Cutting down on advertising, promotions, and development costs of new and emerging markets is a quick way to increase profits in the short term, especially in a recession. Yet when the customer goes to the supermarket, your brand of flour is now on the lower shelf, sitting there, with no advertising. When the recession is over, the customer may have forgotten your brand while the rival product, with its strong marketing over the recession, has now taken top of mind recall. Senior executives wonder why product sales have not grown? They have stopped the life-blood to their products and services. Even in a recession certain activities and processes are still strategic necessities, which must be protected. Yes, these activities have costs, but cost cutting does not mean survival. Marketing expenditure should be treated as a strategic cost to be protected. The focus should be on tracking performance to targets such as market reach, product awareness, and the strength of the distribution channels.

Why Protect Research and Development?

To grow revenues means the organization needs to look at its product range. You need to ask several questions: How much of the revenue base comes from aging products that may be near the end of their product life cycles? How much revenue comes from new and emerging products? It is easy to cut a few million dollars now from the research and development (R&D) budget because this will not affect existing sales or customers. However, in a few years, when the existing products age and customers fall away, the business faces the uphill challenge of catching up with competitors. If having a continual stream of new products is a critical issue, then a target might be that 30% of sales come from new products that are less than 3 years old, as used in 3M. Research and development targets can be important indications of future success (e.g., the number of new products coming into production). They can also provide important indicators of future value.

If tensions exist between using targets for planning, control, and resource allocation, why are budget targets still used for conflicting purposes? Targets in budgets may still be used for evaluation due to their alignment to the annual reporting cycle.[38] Another reason is the use of rolling forecasts enables targets to be set to assist the control function of budgets. By using rolling forecasts, budgets are not out of date but integrated with planning and control purposes. In other words, let us not throw out the "baby with the bath water." We explore this issue in more depth in chapter 7 when we elaborate on the Beyond Budgeting recommendations and how they use different targets for performance evaluation, forecasting, and resource allocation.

Summary

The *art* in target setting is to choose the right level of difficulty in targets when they are set. Getting the right level of target difficulty is challenging because conditions are constantly changing. Difficult choices have to be made. Goal-setting theory argues that specific stretch goals are more motivating than vague goals. Targets that are too difficult or too easy are not motivating. Olympian targets are useful as directional and long-term targets but are not useful for motivational purposes as they can cause gamesmanship, biased forecasts, and, as a result, lost business value. This is the consequence of using budgets as pressure devices over which managers have little control.

Typically organizations set budget targets that are highly achievable, as this has a number of benefits including making managers feel like winners, reducing the control costs, and creating less biased forecasts. In incentive compensation systems, capped performance targets are often used to encourage managers to keep trying to improve performance even if they are likely to just miss the target or to beat the target. However, managers may engage in game playing around the minimum and maximum levels.

Targets are used for multiple and often conflicting purposes. We argue that different targets need to be used for different purposes. For example, motivational targets should be highly achievable with some degree of stretch, whereas targets for planning, coordination, communication, and control need to be at *expected* levels. Setting tight targets for cost reduction can see tensions between cost control and increasing short-term nonfinancial targets (e.g., percentage of new products under three years of age), which will work against the need to protect strategic cost centers such as research and development.

Key Learning Points

- The best performance targets are clear and understandable and give managers the most ability to influence the future (e.g., through clear line of sight). Managers need to have the skill and training to reach the targets. Clear targets that enable learning lead to higher performance than simply urging people to do their best.

- Olympian targets provide direction but are not motivational if they are perceived by people as being unachievable and can result in job-related tension stress, game playing, and fraud.

- Highly achievable targets are generally used to motivate managers for a number of reasons including increasing commitment to goals or creating a winning culture.

- Capped performance targets are used to motivate and reward managers for trying to improve performance even when they will not meet the target or exceed the target. There is often game playing around the minimum and maximum cutoff points.

- Different targets should be used for different purposes. Motivational targets are usually highly achievable (80–90% chance of being reached), whereas targets for planning and forecasting, coordination, and control need to be around what is *expected* to be achieved.

CHAPTER 6

Multiple Performance Targets

You must have long-range goals to keep you from being frustrated by short-range failures.

—Charles C. Noble

Introduction

A long-term view of the business is important in target setting. To lose sight of your long-term strategy can result in short-term actions. No single key performance indicator (KPI) captures all the elements of performance, so use a combination of performance targets that balance the short- and long-term priorities. Karen is a CEO of a company that has focused on financial performance measures in the past but has decided to use multiple performance measures. How many targets should she use? She wonders how to make trade-offs between short- and long-term targets? What are some of the consequences when using multiple performance measures that are not independent of each other? Is it desirable to meet outstanding performance on all targets? Should there be different weights for the targets? These issues are all discussed in the following sections.

Multiple Performance Targets

More companies are using multiple performance targets. Organizations use a variety of financial measures (e.g., profit; earnings before interest, taxes, depreciation, and amortization [EBITDA]; return on assets [ROA]) as well as nonfinancial measures such as inventory levels, labor measures, and quality measures. Using multiple targets may yield several advantages. A combination of targets is likely to capture more aspects of performance. The short-term focus is reduced when targets include lead (forward-looking) KPIs. Another advantage is that multiple targets improve the understanding of the organization's strategy and objectives, especially at lower levels in organizations.[1] Research to date has suggested that nonfinancial measures are selected because of their link to strategy. The nonfinancial measures reflect the drivers of organizational value and play a significant role in strategy development and implementation.[2]

What Is the Right Number of Performance Targets?

One of the biggest challenges for organizations is determining which performance targets to track. If you use too few targets, important aspects of performance may be ignored. If you use too many targets, managers may suffer from information overload and lose focus on the critical performance targets.

Organizations often end up trying to measure too many things. "The result is a wide profusion of peripheral, trivial, or irrelevant measures."[3] A manager of a home finance company that had around 300 measures said, "What I'd really like to know are the 20 measures that tell me how we are really doing."[4] In addition, organizations have hundreds and sometimes thousands of operational measures to choose from. We know that up to a certain point more targets do provide additional information, but after the initial few critical targets, the benefits taper off. The key issue to remember is that just because you can measure something does not mean it becomes a valid performance target.

Information overload from tracking too many performance targets is a major limitation. Using more performance targets does not mean improved decision making because our minds are limited in their ability to process and assimilate the additional data.[5] Busy managers deal with the information overload problem by sifting through the information and identifying what they think is relevant. Some studies have identified that the way evaluators deal with the complexity in performance evaluations is to focus only on a few performance measures that are common across the organization and business units.[6] These common measures are usually financial measures because they are directly comparable across business units and managers. Nonfinancial measures are more likely to be used for performance evaluations of managers and to predict future performance.[7]

The best option seems to be to focus on a few critical targets. If developing new products is a critical issue for your organization, then a good target might be some percentage of sales from new products, as at 3M.[8] An advantage of this approach is that it reduces information overload from tracking too many measures. Using a few critical performance targets is consistent with the Beyond Budgeting approach discussed in the next chapter.

More formal strategic performance measurement systems require major changes in all parts of the organization. One popular system is the balanced scorecard developed by Kaplan and Norton who recommend that strategy be translated into measures and targets that when achieved will mean the successful implementation of strategy.[9] The balanced scorecard develops targets linked to the organizational strategy for four perspectives: financial, customer, internal business processes, and learning and growth. A generic balanced scorecard with objectives and measures is presented in Table 6.1. With four measures recommended for each perspective, at a minimum, a balanced scorecard would have 16 objectives and measures. Targets are then established to enable the monitoring and evaluation of performance to target for each of the 16 measures. However, little advice is given on how to select and weight the performance targets.

Table 6.1. Generic Balanced Scorecard

Financial	Customer
Increase profits (% revenue growth) Increase profits (% cost reduction) Improved asset utilisation (e.g., EVA®) Survival (cash flow)	Increase market share (% increase) Customer acquisition (% increase) Customer satisfaction (% increase) Customer profitability (Increase in customers from targeted segments)
Internal Business Processes	**Learning and Growth**
Innovative processes (e.g., % increase in production from process innovations) Operational excellence (e.g., % increase in production/service efficiency) After sales service (reduction in number of customers requiring after sales service) On-time delivery (% stock delivered on time)	Employee training and development (e.g., number of hours spent on the job training and off site training) Employee satisfaction and motivation (% satisfied and motivated employees) Market development (% marketing spent in new markets) New product development (e.g., % revenue of products developed in last 2 years)

In considering how many targets to use, let us look at some practical issues in terms of monitoring performance. For example, an organization may have six critical performance targets that they are tracking through their monthly reporting systems (see Table 6.2). Using a variance analysis approach for multiple performance targets provides a richer understanding of how and why performance has been achieved. To illustrate the benefits of using visual displays we also use capped targets (e.g., minimum, target, and maximum) as discussed in chapter 5. Table 6.2 illustrates how the performance to the EVA® is very good (around maximum), but this may have been achieved by cost cutting on market development, research and development, and training. Targets for customer satisfaction and health and safety are as expected (on target). The problem is that cutting costs in areas identified as critical KPIs can have important long-term consequences for an organization (as discussed in chapter 5). This information indicates further investigation is needed.

Table 6.2 highlights the performance to six financial and nonfinancial targets. Imagine how complex this table would look if you were tracking 50 targets. How unwieldy would this be for tracking 300 targets!

Having determined how many targets to use, the next important issue is how to determine the weight to be placed on each target. These weights will be used for performance evaluation and rewards.

Table 6.2. Performance to Financial and Nonfinancial Targets

	Minimum	Target	Maximum	Comments
EVA®				
Customer satisfaction				
Market development				
Research and development				
Training				
Health and safety				

How to Weight Targets?

Having the wrong weightings can be just as bad as using the wrong performance measures, as this can impact on the organization's ability to meet its objectives. As Merchant and Van der Stede state, "With the current state of understanding, setting the importance weightings is more of an art than a science. But it is an important art."[10] One reason for this is that the weightings act as a signal from top management on where attention should be focused. For example, the weightings can provide information to managers on how to make decisions such as the trade-off between meeting customer expectations and reducing cost. If profitability received a higher weighting than customer service requirements, managers may interpret this as a signal from top management that reducing costs should take precedence where exceeding customers' service requirements may be a top strategic priority.[11] There are several options to choose from to determine how to weight key measures.

Strategic Importance

A popular approach is to establish the weightings based on the perceived strategic importance of the performance measures.[12] The balanced scorecard is one approach that organizations can use. The idea is to identify causal links between strategy and the key performance measures that need to be reached to successfully implement the strategy.[13] Strategy maps are developed to illustrate how the KPIs link together to implement strategy.

The problem with weightings based on strategic importance is that research shows that managers tend to rely on their gut feelings about what they think is important (e.g., to their customers). A survey shows that fewer than 30% of companies have developed causal models that show how achieving these targets affect future performance.[14] For example, management may be convinced that reducing the time they take to introduce a new product will lead to an increase in market share. However, this may not be the case if the new product is only slightly different from the earlier model.[15] So focusing on meeting the wrong performance targets means that strategy will not be implemented, and this can have serious long-term consequences.

Line of Sight

Another consideration is whether managers have the ability to influence and control the performance to targets, the concept of line of sight we introduced in chapter 1. For example, organization-wide performance targets are often used, despite only the top managers being in a position to influence the targets. Therefore, the behavioral implications of using particular combinations of targets need to be considered.

The perceptions of accuracy and reliability of particular measures can also impact on the weightings. Financial measures have their limitations including that they are noisy, inaccurate, incomplete, and often are poor proxies of performance.[16] There are also problems with nonfinancial measures as they may be hard to quantify, and it can be difficult to get reliable data (e.g., customer satisfaction surveys).[17] Some evidence shows there is often a higher emphasis on nonfinancial measures when accounting performance measures are inaccurate.[18] While companies may track a number of financial and nonfinancial measures, they may not use them in decision making for evaluation and rewards if they are seen as inaccurate and unreliable.

Evidence shows managers also play games to achieve nonfinancial performance targets. The weightings on performance measures could be chosen because these are the measures that managers think they are more likely to achieve or adjust. The targets for nonfinancial performance measures may be made more achievable by changing the measures or lowering the performance target.[19] One bank linked employee bonuses to the results of a customer satisfaction survey. However, the bank only surveyed customers who went into the branches, so a branch manager who had low customer satisfaction scores in the past decided to improve his scores by offering customers free food and drink.[20]

Long- and Short-Term Targets

Long-term and short-term time horizons also need to be considered when weighting performance measures. We recommend you use a combination of targets that include a focus on both past performance (e.g., financial performance measures) and lead indicators (e.g., market share, warranty claims) that provide some indication of future performance.

Let us consider the example of Karen, a CEO who comes back from a leadership course and decides that she will set the objectives and targets for one of her business units. She tells the business unit manager that she wants a 5% revenue growth with a 7% cost reduction and a 12% growth in EVA®. The business unit manager talks to the other senior managers in the business unit, and they examine how they could achieve this. The financial targets (e.g., revenue, cost, EVA®) are lag indicators, and so the focus needs to be on identifying lead indicators.

How can the business unit increase revenue, reduce costs, and increase profitability in the future? The business unit needs to be more innovative (e.g., more or better products and services that have increased value in the eyes of the customer), and operations need to be more efficient (e.g., reduced costs without losing value in the eyes of the customer, enhanced supply chains). The problem is investing in innovations or process improvements can reduce the financial measures in the short-term. In addition, the easiest way to increase the financial measures is to take short-term actions such as cutting discretionary expenditure such as research and development, marketing, and employee training. The reasons for protecting marketing, research and development, and employee training are discussed in chapter 5. These are lead indicators of future performance, and they will take time to yield the financial benefits Karen requires.

To avoid taking a short-term focus, you need to take into account the different time horizons. The best way to address this is to adjust the financial targets in the short term and increase them when the payoff from the nonfinancial performance kicks in. The problem is that few organizations do this.[21]

Weightings in Incentive Compensation

The weightings used in incentive compensation systems are important because they are designed to motivate managers to meet the most important targets and get the rewards. A useful rule of thumb is not to include any measure in incentive compensation if it not weighted at least 5–10% of base salary.[22] The issue here is that when using multiple performance measures the 5–10% rule of thumb would not be possible except for the most senior managers where the bonus pool is very high.[23] The problem is that placing low weightings on any measure in evaluation and incentives can mean managers may give little attention to achieving the performance target. People may perceive that reaching the target is just not worth the effort! For example, an Australasian organization used a balanced scorecard-type incentive system where 85% of the organization's performance was based on financial measures (and primarily EVA®) and 15% was placed on the nonfinancial measures.[24] While top management's attention was to highlight the importance of the nonfinancial measures, the low weightings signaled that they were relatively unimportant.

Despite the increasing use of multiple targets, short-term financial measures remain heavily weighted in incentive compensation systems.[25] This is not surprising because of the pressure from analysts and the stock markets in the United States and the United Kingdom have focused executives' attention on the financial numbers.[26] Case Capsule 6.1 shows how the financial targets received the highest weightings, despite the importance and use of nonfinancial measures.

Having determined the weights on particular targets, the next question is do you reward performance if only some of the performance targets have been achieved? What if five critical performance targets are linked to incentive compensation, but only three of the five targets are achieved? Do all the five performance targets need to be achieved, or do managers still get part of the bonus for achieving some three out of the five performance targets? There is no perfect answer to these questions. One possible solution would be to calculate the incentive payment by multiplying the percentage achieved by the weights for the targets. The key issue is to understand the behavioral implications of the choices you make. By weighting certain target more than others, managers may focus on the more important targets and not address the lesser-weighted targets.

The choice of weightings needs to be carefully considered as it can lead managers to play games to maximize their rewards. One option to overcome this problem is to reward managers for various levels of performance using capped targets, as illustrated earlier in Table 6.2 (for more information on capped targets, see chapter 5). Another way to overcome this issue is to introduce some subjectivity into the evaluation process (see chapter 3). Having discussed how to select and weight performance

Case Capsule 6.1. Weightings of Targets in a Balanced Scorecard Incentive System

A U.S. study has examined the balanced scorecard implementation in Global Financial Services (a pseudonym used to ensure confidentiality for the organization) and has been showcased by Kaplan and Norton. Despite the use of multiple performance measures that included lead indicators linked to strategy, financial measures remained heavily weighted in performance evaluations. Evaluators focused on financial measures because they had discretion over the choice and weight of the measures. The organization had also emphasized the financial measures in the prior incentive compensation plan. A major problem with the emphasis on financial measures was that other KPIs that were important lead indicators were ignored.

An internal survey of managers at Global Financial Services found that while most managers understood the balanced scorecard process and their targets, only 32% were satisfied with the overall balanced scorecard process.[27] In relation to performance evaluation and bonuses, the managers held a range of views on the fairness of the balanced scorecard (31% agreed, 48% disagreed) and on whether the bonuses reflected differences in performance (30% agreed, 35% disagreed). Targets were perceived as being realistic (40% agreed, 33% disagreed), and there were mixed responses to whether the balanced scorecard targets covered all the important aspects of the job (39% agreed, 40% disagreed). Following managers' complaints of biases such as favoritism in the bonus allocations and the lack of clarify on the evaluation criteria, the incentive compensation plan was subsequently abandoned.

targets, we now consider some of the consequences when performance targets are not independent of each other.

How Do the Targets Interact With Each Other?

Multiple targets are often not independent of each other, which means that they interact in different ways: They can be substitutes for each other, may complement each other, or may be destructive to one another. One example is the relationship between production output and labor productivity. Employees can work harder and this increases output, but employees at some stage can get tired and burnt out.[28]

Some targets are substitutes for each other. For example, profitability can be measured by return on investment, return on capital employed, and earnings before interest and tax. While each of these financial targets has subtle differences, focusing on this set only generates a set of measures that can be substitutes. Therefore you need to choose the measures that are the best proxies, rather than using several measures that capture the same aspects of performance. This reduces the number of targets that need to be tracked.

Some targets are complements for each other. The advantage of using a combination of financial and nonfinancial targets is that this improves the information available to measure performance. This is often called the *informativeness principle*, which argues that measures should be added as long as they provide additional information on performance.[29] The additional information helps address the problem that important information is lost when information is aggregated into financial measures. The key issue here is to focus on the critical targets that provide incremental information; otherwise this also leads to information overload.

In some cases the tension between the targets can be destructive for the organization. The dilemma many companies face is hoping that managers will focus on the long term, even though their evaluation and rewards are based on short-term performance. This is the classic argument, "On the folly of rewarding for A while hoping for B."[30] To avoid targets being destructive, you need to take into account the different time horizons, as discussed earlier in this chapter.

What Happens If There Are Diminishing Returns?

Outstanding performance in all areas of business is not always desirable. It can result in diminishing returns to the organization. One organization set a target of 100% for customer satisfaction. The problem was on further analysis they found that the customers who were 80% satisfied spent the same amount of money with the firm as those who were 100% satisfied.[31] This shows that there may be little payoff (or even a negative effect) from over investing by making customers 100% satisfied.

Let us look at a couple of examples of how to analyze customer profitability so you have the necessary data to set performance targets.

Setting Targets for Customers: Know Your Customer

The adage of attracting and retaining customers is legendary folklore for business success. Let us return to the example of Karen, the CEO who has set a business unit target at a 5% increase in revenue. Before establishing the performance targets, the business unit managers need to analyze what their customers need and want. They should also identify the highly profitable customers they want to retain and build relationships with. It is useful to understand the profitability of customers over a long-term horizon. Some customers who are unprofitable in the short term grow to be profitable in the long term (e.g., university students for banks). Unprofitable customers need to be managed so that high costs such as the number of set ups and capacity fluctuations are reduced. By managing these costs and tracing them to the customer types, managers can charge certain customer groups extra for late scheduled orders. The pricing structure may need to be changed so that discounts are given to customers whose orders are well scheduled and require low set ups.

Pareto's law is a useful technique to analyze your customers. In relation to customer profitability analysis, typically 80% of the profitability comes from 20% of the customers. The next 70% of the customers are about break even while the remaining 10% of customers lose around 50% to 200% of the profits. The issue here is do you keep only the top 20% of customers, keep the top 20% and middle 70% of customers, or keep all of them and try to manage their profitability? This relationship is illustrated in the following Figure 6.1.

Case Capsule 6.2 examines the use of a grid, which is useful to analyze customer profitability to assist in setting performance targets.

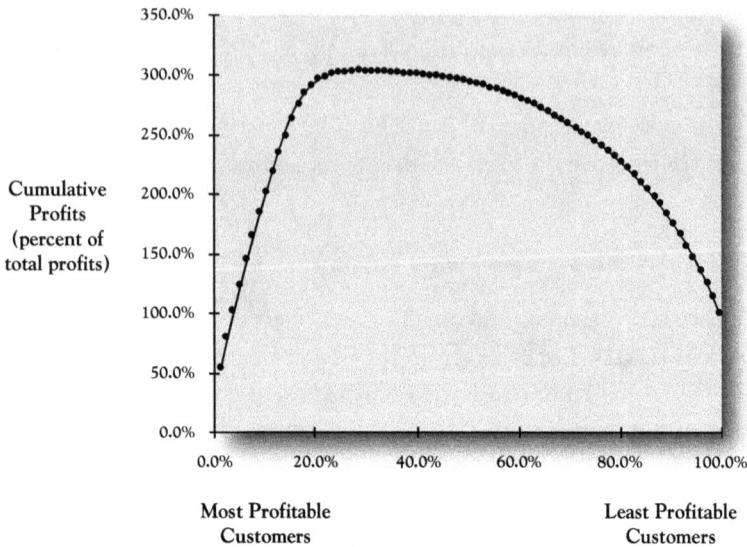

Figure 6.1. Whale curve of cumulative profitability.

Case Capsule 6.2. Customer Profitability Grid

The customer profitability grid is a technique that traces costs through the products to the customer. This example of customer profitability analysis is from a small plastics container manufacturer.[32] Four clusters of customers are identified. Customer types labeled as B and C place regular orders and give large lead times for manufacturing. The setup of the plastic molding machinery was not difficult, and the printing was specified to standard product lines. Clearly they were winners. Customer A was a new, large order customer who varied the product specification, gave very short lead times for manufacturing with resulting overtime, and large set ups of the molding and injection machines. Customer D is an irregular customer who often changes the product specification at the last minute. Figure 6.2 illustrates where these four types of customers (A, B, C, and D) are located on the customer profitability grid.

This small plastic container manufacturer had two principal owners; Steve was gifted in marketing while Earl was the operations

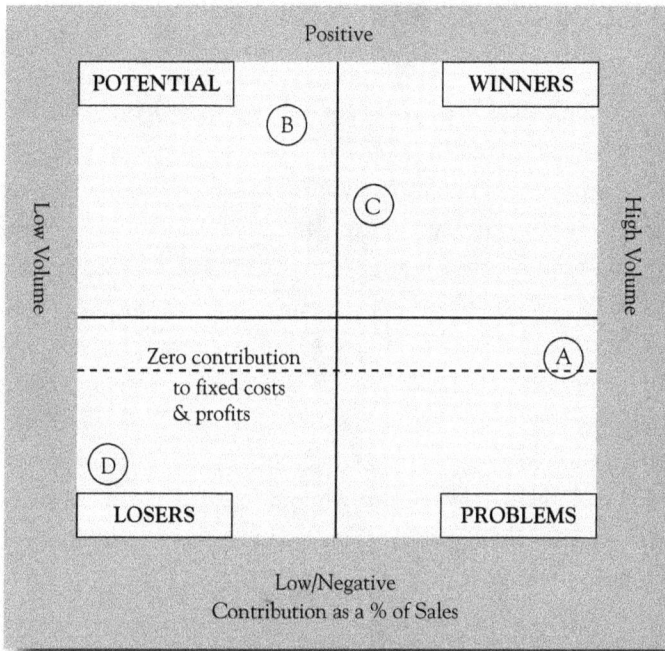

Figure 6.2. Customer profitability grid.

specialist. When the results of the customer profitability analysis were presented to the manufacturer, Earl sat down at the start of the meeting, stating that he was a busy man and could only stay for 15 minutes, whereas Steve said that he would sit through the whole presentation. As the results of the customer profitability analysis were discussed, Earl decided not to leave. He was an engineer and was amazed that accounting was now talking his language, namely, set ups, product complexity, and diversity. In relation to Customer A, Earl jumped up and said, "I told you, this customer just drains us, yes. This customer is the largest we have, but we work overtime to that schedule." The situation was changed. Steve, the marketing expert, was now questioning and challenging the analysis. Steve could not stand the thought of letting Customer A go. Earl did not leave for the 3 hours of the presentation but would only interject occasionally "I agree on this point." The purpose of the analysis was not to suggest getting rid of any customers, rather just to point out that activity-based costing (ABC) of customers could identify resources consumed (we elaborate on ABC in chapter 7). The strategic decision of keeping or eliminating any customer had to consider not only the short-term value of the customer but also the lifetime value.

This customer profitability analysis is focused on identifying which customers will result in revenue growth as well as an increase in profits. If the organization gains a lot of customer type D, then revenues will increase from the financial perspective, but this will not increase profits. Getting one large customer A also will increase revenue but not profits or EVA®. The gold mine is retaining and winning more of customer types B and C. Those customers (B and C) do not increase costs, consume few support resources, are regular in their product ordering, and, finally, pay on time without fuss. Give them the corporate box seats for the high-profile games, treat them with kid gloves, and do not let a competitor near them.

Instead of setting targets in isolation, the earlier discussion highlights the importance of conducting some analysis into the factors (e.g., know your customer) affecting the critical performance targets that will ensure organizational objectives are achieved.

Summary

Multiple performance targets are used to ensure organizations are focused on the longer-term strategic priorities, as well as meeting short-term targets. Using a combination of targets captures more elements of performance, provides additional information, and improves decision making. Focusing on a few critical targets is better than trying to monitor performance to 300 targets. The reason is that too many targets are unwieldy and lead to information overload.

Deciding how much weight to place on multiple performance targets is more of an *art than a science*.[33] It is crucial to get it right as there can be serious long-term consequences from getting it wrong. The *art* is making the right choices in terms of balancing strategic importance, line of sight (e.g., ability to influence, accuracy), and short- and long-term time horizons. Targets used for incentive compensation systems need to receive weightings that will result in managers making the right choices in terms of balancing strategic importance, and the rewards need to be high enough to get the attention of managers.

Using a combination of performance targets also requires an understanding of how the measures interact with each other. Some measures may be redundant as they are measuring the same things. Other measures may be complementary as they provide information on different aspects of performance. While the combination of some measures may be destructive, such as focusing on short-term measures when longer-term performance is desired. Desiring outstanding performance in all areas can lead to diminishing returns such as whether it is worth achieving a target of 100% customer satisfaction?

The best approach is to use a combination of short-term financial measures (lag indicators), together with some good leading indicators of future performance.[34] One must bear in mind the quote at the start of the chapter, that not achieving short-term targets is not failure. Rather keeping an eye on the long-term horizon and managing short-term KPIs, which lead to longer-term future performance, is indeed a delicate balancing act.

Key Learning Points

- Multiple targets for financial and nonfinancial measures are being used because they balance short- and long-term priorities, capture different elements of performance, help track strategy implementation, and improve decision making.
- Focus on a few critical targets, and no more than the 16–20 targets recommended for the balanced scorecard.
- Weightings can be determined by the importance of the measures to strategic initiatives, line of sight (e.g., reliability), and short- versus long-term priorities.
- You need to understand how your choice of weightings will influence managers' behaviors.
- Individual targets used in incentive compensation plans should be worth around 5–10% of base salary to get the attention of managers.

- Understand how the performance measures interact with each other (e.g., substitutes, complements, destroys).
- Conduct sensitivity analysis so you know how changing conditions will affect performance and avoid diminishing returns.

CHAPTER 7

Innovations in Target Setting

If you find it difficult to accept failure then you simply won't get any innovation because employees will be too frightened.

—Sir Terry Leahy (former CEO of Tesco)

Introduction

"Budgets are time consuming and irrelevant to the strategic management of my business." "Budgets are out of date in a rapidly changing environment and are just a game for accountants to play." These views are common and valid as often a budget is just last year's numbers tinkered with so that managers can get on with the real business of generating value.

We examine two recent innovations in target setting: activity-based budgeting and the Beyond Budgeting approach. Activity-based budgeting advocates argue that budgets should be more closely connected to operations and process improvement. In contrast, the Beyond Budgeting group proposes that the annual, fixed budget-setting process should abolished and replaced with a new management approach that includes empowerment, rolling forecasts, and relative performance evaluation. These innovative ideas to improve budgeting require changes in the way performance is managed in organizations. The Leahy quote sums up the challenge for managers—to accept that it can be a trial-and-error process to implement innovative practices.

Why Are Companies Looking at New Ways to Improve the Budgeting Process?

Just about every article you read on budgeting talks about problems: Budgets are static and out of date as soon as they are prepared; budgets are focused on financial control rather than strategic and operational control. Managers find it difficult to use this information to manage their businesses. By the time the actual quarter results are out and compared to the budget, you are well into the next quarter. Budgets are outdated. In addition, linking fixed budgets to performance evaluations and incentives often results in managers attempting to game the system, and these actions usually have detrimental impacts on the organization. Here are some of the growing criticisms of budgeting:[1]

1. Budgets are time consuming and costly to put together.
2. Budgets constrain responsiveness and flexibility and are often a barrier to change.
3. Budgets are rarely strategically focused and are often contradictory.
4. Budgets add little value, especially given the time required to prepare them.
5. Budgets concentrate on cost reduction and not on value creation.
6. Budgets strengthen vertical command and control systems.
7. Budgets do not reflect the emerging network structures that organizations are adopting.
8. Budgets encourage *gaming* and perverse behaviors.
9. Budgets are developed and updated too infrequently, usually annually.
10. Budgets are based on unsupported assumptions and guesswork.
11. Budgets reinforce departmental barriers rather than encourage knowledge sharing.
12. Budgets make people feel undervalued.

One of the ideas that have been proposed to improve budgeting is the activity-based budgeting approach.

Activity-Based Budgeting

Activity-based budgeting is an innovative approach to budgeting that starts at the operational level and links *operations* with the *financial numbers*. It is future orientated as it helps identify what processes, activities and costs should be in the future. Activity-based budgeting builds on the concepts of activity-based costing (ABC). Activity-based budgeting is an attempt to combine process improvement with product costing and financial management. The activity-based budgeting approach is useful in manufacturing and service organizations to highlight inefficiencies, bottlenecks, and resourcing needs and to improve communication at the lower levels by providing a better link between operations and financial numbers.

The next section provides a brief overview of *time-driven* activity-based costing to provide the necessary background to understand how *time-driven* activity-based budgeting has developed.

What Is *Time-Driven* Activity-Based Costing?

ABC is one of the most innovative developments in costing in the past century. It is an attempt to completely change the way companies cost products and services. ABC has promoted different ways of thinking about costing and has received a lot of attention by the business schools and practitioners. ABC is included in most textbooks on costing, and numerous consultancy businesses sell the ABC concept.[2]

Kaplan and Anderson have recently proposed time-driven ABC to simplify the process while still getting the main benefits of the ABC system. The aim is to address some of the limitations of ABC, which was seen as too expensive to develop and maintain, took too long to implement, and did not capture the complexity of the operations.[3] In contrast, managers taking a time-driven approach use their own estimates (e.g., resource demands for transactions and activities) in order to overcome the problems with getting employees to identify the time spent on all their activities. Time-driven ABC focuses on two issues: "the cost per time unit of supplying the resource capacity and the unit times of consumption of the resource capacity."[4] The steps required are as follows:

1. Estimate the time employees spend on various activities, focusing on practical capacity (typically estimated around 80–85% of the time).

2. Estimate the time involved in completing one unit of each of the activities.

3. Calculate the cost driver rates by multiplying the result in steps 1 and 2.

The main idea is that time-driven ABC provides the missing link between operations and the balanced scorecard.[5] Kaplan and Norton recommend using time-driven ABC to assist with resource capacity planning and to help organizations estimate what resources they will need to implement their strategic plans. The process involves using past trends to make estimates about resource usage to assess capacity (what the requirements are), leading to an estimate of capacity utilization. The lack of operational focus and ignoring capacity issues has been a limitation of the balanced scorecard.

The benefits of time-driven ABC are that it is a more simplified version of ABC and easier to develop because it calls for less involvement of lower level employees to specify their activities and more estimates by senior managers. The emphasis of time-driven ABC is to get better estimates, recognizing that accurate costing is not possible until after the period being analyzed. As with all costing systems, however, time-driven ABC is still complex and costly to establish and maintain. Also, there has been little independent research to assess the benefits and implementation issues of adoption of time-driven ABC.

How Does Activity-Based Budgeting Work?

Activity-based budgeting (ABB) has been developed by Cooper and Kaplan to change the focus from costing to linking ABC to operational budgets.[6] ABB links operations and costing because it focuses on planning and controlling value-adding activities and processes.

Taking a time-driven approach to ABB provides another way to decide on the future resources needed to meet forecasted sales and production. The focus is on identifying resource usage and capacity of processes and activities, not line items as in traditional budgeting.[7] Kaplan and Anderson's time-driven ABB approach is to analyze all activities and processes and to make decisions as to what costs are going to be covered in the period. It is an adaption of zero-based budgeting approach, rather than assuming that most costs are fixed in the short term (as discussed in chapter 4). They provide an example of a fictitious case called Sippican Corporation to illustrate the benefits of ABB. These are the steps they recommend taking:

1. Develop the ABC model from most recent experience.
2. Calculate product, service, and customer profitability. *What if* analyses are very useful to make these predictions. This step is important because the analysis undertaken earlier will show what resource capabilities are needed in the future, rather than simply using existing capabilities only.
3. Consider options for process improvement, pricing, sales, and product mixes, and so forth. The analysis focuses around understanding how to improve profitability.
4. Forecast future capabilities of processes and consider different scenarios to analyze the impact of different combinations of sales and purchases that will improve performance. Enterprise resource planning systems are available to do this type of analysis.
5. Forecast the future demand for the resource capacity. This builds on the previous analysis of volume and sales mix. ABB can also include *buffers* so that resources can be adjusted upward or downward for changes in sales or production.
6. Review and authorize spending for the future period's resource requirements.

The following case capsule provides a simple example that shows how activity-based budgeting is different from traditional budgeting.

Case Capsule 7.1. Traditional Budgeting Versus Activity-Based Budgeting

This example from an insurance company shows how the activity-based budget is more meaningful and easier to understand and manage, compared to the traditional budget.[8]

The traditional budget is organized around line items for each of the expenses incurred by the insurance company (see Table 7.1).

How does the traditional budget compare to an activity-based budget? As noted earlier, time-driven activity-based budgeting requires managers to use their own estimates of the time taken for all the activities and processes the insurance company does, taking into account any changes that are going to be made. The result of the analysis is the cost per unit and the resource capacity usage of the activity (see Table 7.2).

Table 7.1. The Traditional Budget Approach

Expenses	Budget
Salaries and wages	$650,000
Benefits	$195,000
Rent	$52,000
Supplies	$78,000
Computing	$65,000
Travel and accommodation	$39,000
Consultancy	$91,000
Telephone	$24,505
Total expenses	**$1,194,505**

Table 7.2. The Activity-Based Budget

Activity	Cost per unit	Usage	Activity cost
Processing mail	.26	23,000	$5,980
Initial review	$20	23,000	$460,000
Professional review	$57	1,150	$65,550
Adjuster review	$35	2,300	$80,500
Explanation of benefits memorandum	$10	23,000	$230,000
Writing checks	$7	13,800	$96,600
Answering questions	$5	11,500	$57,500
Dispute resolution	$345	575	$198,375
Managing department			**$1,194,505**

Case Capsule 7.2 describes an ABB implementation and the implementation issues raised here explain why Kaplan and colleagues are promoting the simpler *time-driven* ABB approach.

Case Capsule 7.2. Sierra Trucks

This case examines the consultancy-based implementation of activity-based budgeting in Sierra Trucks in the Midwest United States.[9] The features of this implementation are that the company had been using activity-based costing for some time, the costs were considered reliable, and that it involved enterprise resource planning (ERP) consultants. Implementing ABB requires a more complex understanding of the drivers causing the costs than ABC. Therefore, data collection was extensive (e.g., customer data, process flows) and required rigorous review and checking of the data by the ABB team and the process owners. The data was analyzed to understand the relationships between the variables, to emphasize the need to understand actual usage (rather than capacity), and to identify bottlenecks for resources and activities. They have used different approaches to ABB implementation in the three different areas, which included a) translating the ABC system to activity-based budgeting, b) creating a new ABB system, and c) a combination of the two. The benefits were improved operational reporting, better understanding of the relationships between costs and work flows, improved costing, and the ability to evaluate the impact of various scenarios (e.g., volume, sales mix). Because ABB takes a "back to front" approach to ABC and is forward looking and predictive, they had the most problems when trying to make predictions using the ABC system. They found that converting the activity-based costing model to activity-based budgeting was the most technically challenging part of the process.

Activity-based budgeting links operations to the financial numbers, and the benefits include that ABB matches resource demands with unused capacity; provides important operational information enabling monitoring of actual usage and spending against budgets. It also gives managers more control over their cost structure, for example, the traditional fixed costs, such as equipment, people, and facilities. ABB also takes an important step towards improving budgeting by focusing on resource constraints, capacity utilization, and capital allocations at the operational level—before preparing the financial budgets. ABB information provides managers with information they can use to plan, coordinate, monitor, and control their operations, rather than looking at the type of costs or line items usually presented in traditional budgets.

Activity-based budgeting information together with the use of enterprise resource planning systems enable *what if* analysis and scenario analysis on the impact of different mixes of sales, activities, and capacity. This information enables managers to work backwards from forecasts for sales and production in order to work out the activities needed and to ensure resources are available to meet the needs of these activities.

While *time-driven* ABB is in its early development, some types of organizations would benefit from this approach. For example, ABB may be more useful in stable operating environments rather than those involved in innovative or flexible environments.[10] While most of the ABB implementations seem to be in manufacturing, advocates believe that service organizations could benefit from ABB as well. Organizations who match these requirements are more likely to benefit from activity-based budgeting that is

- customer focused;
- focused on process improvement;
- aimed at a better understanding of processes and activities that drive costs;
- aimed at understanding why resource usage is important;
- engaged in creating transparency about costs, usage, and capacity of operations;
- open to input from employees at all levels;
- committed in terms of time and investment.

While the ABB and balanced scorecard advocates have focused on making budgets more contemporary, another group advocates the abandonment of budgets.

Beyond Budgeting and No Budgets

The Beyond Budgeting Roundtable Group recommends the development of a new management model, which focuses around four areas, including leadership, radical decentralization, rolling forecasts, and relative performance evaluation with the benefit of hindsight.[11] The Beyond Budgeting Roundtable was initially formed as part of the Consortium of Advanced Management, International (CAM-I) by Jeremy Hope and Robin Fraser in 1997 and they have around 100 companies as members.[12] They have contributed to the budgeting debate by showcasing some companies that have cut the link between budget targets and incentive compensation, starting with the approach championed by Jan Wallander, CEO of Svenska Handelsbanken (a Swedish bank), in the 1970s.[13]

Different Targets for Different Purposes

The Beyond Budgeting approach to target setting is to have separate targets for: performance evaluation, forecasting, and resource allocation process (as elaborated on in chapter 5).[14] They argue that this avoids the problems in traditional budgeting systems where managers tend to manipulate the forecasts as they know they are going to be used for resource allocation, evaluation, and rewards. Traditional forecasts are so biased that they cannot be used for predicting the future. In contrast, the Beyond Budgeting proponents argue that performance targets need to be ambitious and longer-term focused, whereas forecasts should reflect expected outcomes and signal when problems need corrective action.[15] (We discuss forecasting techniques in chapter 4.)

Relative Performance Targets

Relative performance evaluation is the benchmark used for a range of key performance indicators (KPIs), such as profit and customer satisfaction. These relative performance targets are either benchmarked internally (e.g., with teams or branches in the same company) or externally (e.g., with leading competitors). Performance targets are expected to be achieved in the medium term. The target-setting approach is based around continuous improvement and giving managers a reasonable period of time to meet the benchmarks. The managers at Borealis (an innovative provider of plastics solutions) argue they use ABC systems, and the result of their extensive benchmarking process is that performance targets are usually tougher than when they were negotiated.[16] League tables are also used to publicize the rankings to provide a competitive spirit to encourage people to make improvements in their operations to improve their rankings.

Having good comparative data is important. In the Svenska Handelsbanken they use relative KPIs to compare performance across regions and business areas.[17] However, finding good relative data can be difficult. In Statoil where it is difficult to measure market share percentages, they use market share rankings, and production regularity percentages can be replaced with internal league tables if there are no external peers. If benchmarking data is not available, Statoil uses past performance.[18] We elaborated on the issues with external and internal benchmarking and relative performance targets in chapter 4.

Rolling Forecasts

The use of rolling forecasts is to map out *expected* future performance. Focus on a few critical KPIs (e.g., orders, sales, costs, profits, cash flows) so the organization can get a quick forecast of what is predicted to happen. The rolling forecasts are continually updated every few months (usually quarterly) and cover the same period (usually 5–8 quarters ahead) (as shown in chapter 3). There is no finish line, and so the forecasts are more accurate as they are constantly updated with recent events. Learning is important. In addition, planning is more accurate as the forecasts are not biased. The reason is that under the Beyond Budgeting approach the forecasts are disconnected from performance targets and resource allocation processes, as discussed earlier.[19] The performance targets for KPIs are not specially linked to the forecasts, and so the gap between the targeted performance and the forecasts needs to be investigated and managed. In Borealis, for example, they use rolling five-quarter forecasts for a range of performance targets including return on capital, profit, and volumes.[20] Managers argue that the forecasts are more accurate since they are not linked to performance evaluation and incentive compensation.

Resourcing

Strategy is everyone's business, and strategic planning is informal and continual. Resourcing the strategic initiatives is critical. Beyond Budgeting

organizations have processes to fast track operational and capital investment funding processes to enable strategic opportunities to be taken
quickly, rather than waiting for the next annual planning round. This
means that resources are available on a timely basis. Key performance
indicators are aligned to strategy, and regular performance reviews identify risks and opportunities.

The aim here is to give managers boundaries that provide the flexibility they need to operate effectively, providing processes that allow
for fast tracking major projects and delegating responsibility for smaller
projects. Rather than the "spend it or lose it" mentality that is promoted
by the traditional budgeting, they make funds available to managers as
the resources are required. This reduces managers' need to put up buffers
(e.g., slack).[21] Interestingly, Bogsnes, who was in charge of the Beyond
Budgeting implementation at Borealis, argues that costs actually reduced
when they abandoned budgets in 1996, partly because people took more
responsibility for their actions.[22]

To illustrate how forecasts can be disconnected from the targets used
for performance evaluation and resource allocation, a case of a Norwe-
gian oil company, Statoil, is presented in Case Capsule 7.3.

Case Capsule 7.3. Statoil

In 2007, Statoil became the world's largest offshore energy producer,
the world's third largest seller of crude oil, and Europe's second largest
gas supplier. Statoil was also the largest company based in Scandi-
navia, measured by market capitalization (nearly US$70 billion),
annual sales (US$68 billion), and a net operating income (US$6.5
billion). The company employed 30,000 people in 42 countries. The
Statoil organizational structure was relatively flat. It consisted of six
main business units—(1) Development and Production–Norway, (2)
Development and Production–International, (3) Natural Gas, (4)
Manufacturing and Marketing, (5) Projects and Procurement, and (6)
Technology and New Energy.[23] In 2011, a new business unit, Development and Production–North America, was added.

Target Difficulty in Statoil

Statoil wanted managers to define KPIs that were relative, rather than absolute targets. The relative KPIs linked inputs with outputs (e.g., cost per barrel) and, where possible, they compared the organization's performance with external and internal benchmarks. The relative KPI targets were considered more robust, objective, and had the added advantage that they did not need to be continuously updated. Statoil motivated employees by comparing their performance relative to their peers and encouraging sharing best practices and learning from the top performers. In terms of the level of target difficulty, Geir Slora (Senior Vice President, Drilling and Well) clarified, "We want achievement of the targets to be possible. In most cases we are not aiming at world records. We are aiming at being in the top 25%."[24]

Statoil recognised that there was no perfect KPI or set of KPIs. Instead they were aware that the KPIs were only indicators of how strategy implement was going. Rather than focusing solely on the targets, they focused more on what was the objective they were trying to achieve and what actions they needed to take to implement strategy.

Competing Purposes of Budget Targets

Their traditional budgeting process required them to use one set of budget numbers for a range of competing purposes including target setting, forecasting and resource allocation. The budget target when also used as a forecast became biased because the same number also served as a motivational target, and for resource allocation. They argue that a stretch sales target used to motivate employees cannot be the same number as the forecasted level of sales needed for planning and coordination purposes. Statoil managers have developed different targets for different purposes to improve the quality of each of the targets.

Targets set for motivational purposes were both stretch and relative to other organizations (external targets) or internal targets such as the Health, Safety, & Environment measure of "Serious Incident Frequency" commonly used in the exploration areas within Statoil. Relative performance targets provided several advantages. As this avoided the problems with negotiating targets annually, they found managers set more ambitious targets for themselves to avoid being seen as a *shirker* and it encouraged managers to learn from other areas who were performing better on a relative basis.

Forecasts are based around what outcomes are expected. The forecasts are used for planning and coordination purposes as they are continually updated so that the latest forecasts (called rolling forecasts) indicate the level of performance that is expected to be achieved. The forecasts are also designed to provide early warnings of problems that might be occurring so that corrective actions can be taken. The advantage of the Statoil approach was that these standalone forecasts were not subject to the typical biases with budget targets used for evaluation and the allocation of rewards.

Statoil's forecasts reflected the *expected* level of performance. From 2010, Statoil has used what they call dynamic (or event-based) forecasting and target setting. Bjarte Bogsnes explained that, "An event is either something that happens around us or an action we take ourselves that has an effect that should be reflected in our targets and forecasts."[25] Forecasts are continuously updated when significant events or new information is received. Local managers update minor changes to their forecasts in a log for everyone to see in the management information system. Major changes that require the forecasts to be changed need senior management approval. This means that everyone is aware of the impact of recent events on the forecasts; changes can be made when needed rather than waiting for the annual budgeting cycle.

The resource allocation process at Statoil was also disconnected from the annual budget. Resources were still allocated for strategic projects or major capital investment decisions at the time when the resources were required, rather than waiting for an annual approval process. "The bank is open year round," Bjarte Bogsnes exclaimed, "but you can still get a no on your request for money."[26] The intention of Statoil's continuous resource allocation process was to change managers' mind-set away from focusing on whether there were resources in the budget for strategic initiatives, to whether this investment was the right decision to make.

Clearly, Statoil has established a continuous program that questions the role of the traditional budget. Bogsnes, a senior executive in Statoil and part of the Beyond Budgeting movement, argues that using the same target for evaluation, resource allocation, and forecasting is guaranteed to destroy the quality of the forecast. The Statoil case highlights that the purpose the targets are being used for needs to be considered when deciding the level of difficulty required in the target, and the time horizon (e.g., performance targets require a medium-term horizon). Bogsnes claimed that Statoil "abolished the budget in 2005."[27] However, budgets are still required by Statoil's external partners for large projects, which is confusing for managers.[28] Clearly, managers who did not use budgets for internal purposes now had to prepare and rely on budgets for external partners for large and strategic projects. One senior manager notes, "It is hard to be dynamic if our partners are not also dynamic. Most of them want to see an annual budget."[29] Perhaps the view that Statoil and the Beyond Budgeting advocates are more dynamic than their partners warrants attention.

The Beyond Budgeting advocates provide little advice on how to select measures (and gain agreement from employees), how to set the targets, how to manage the implications of different levels in target difficulty, how the measures should be weighted, and how to link them to incentive compensation. The examples given in their case studies take different approaches.

In addition to the technical changes, Beyond Budgeting requires a change in the mind-set of managers.

Radical Decentralization

Fundamental to the Beyond Budgeting approach is what they call radical decentralization, that is, empowering employees to promote a high performance climate. This requires changing an organization's performance management philosophy and processes towards using relative KPIs, tighter target setting through internal and external benchmarking, continuous monitoring of KPIs, continuous improvement of processes, and empowering employees. Beyond Budgeting organizations have baseline performance expectations for KPIs, and financial information is distributed frequently and openly with the focus on trends rather than actual figures. Financial budgets are still used by the Chief Financial Officer, but are kept at that level for managing cash flows and financial control; they are not used in performance evaluation and rewards.[30] There is also more monitoring and control at the front line and across the interrelated parts of the organization. While radical decentralization empowered managers to strive for excellence, a related issue is how to evaluate and reward performance.

How Are Relative Performance Targets Used for Evaluation and Rewards?

Performance to relative targets is done with the *benefit of hindsight* using information available at the end of the period, although managers will know in advance which performance targets they will be assessed on. The idea is that performance evaluation will be based on actual operating conditions and the economic circumstances faced in the period. This means that people are evaluated on their performance relative to their peers who had to deal with the similar issues (e.g., currency, interest rates, oil prices). The Beyond Budgeting advocates relate this to a car race, where everyone knows what is expected, but the results are not known until the end.

The relative performance contract requires employees to trust senior management to fairly assess their performance by peer review based on a manager's performance compared to peers, and with the benefit of hindsight.[31] The relative performance evaluation may be challenging to implement because it relies on getting benchmarks that are agreed upon and considered fair.[32] It is also important that managers have a clear line of sight so that they understand the criteria they are being evaluated on, what performance standards are expected, and how they can influence the performance targets (see chapter 1).

Evidence has shown that the use of relative performance targets for incentive compensation is increasing.[33] However, there is little practical advice on the best way to do this. For example, the Beyond Budgeting case studies all take different approaches to setting performance targets and linking them to incentive compensation. Some firms provide a preagreed formula that shows the weightings to be attached to different measures for performance evaluation and incentive compensation. Rhodia, a large chemical company, used a combination of individual, business unit, and company performance measures. Svenska Handelsbanken, a Swedish bank, used a company-wide plan and league tables to keep the pressure on continue improvement. The profit-sharing plan at this bank pays bonuses into a pension fund, and the bonuses are not paid out until retirement or the person leaves the firm. At Statoil all employees have individual performance goals that cascade down the levels, as well as annual and biannual reviews. This is similar to personal scorecards or Management by Objectives (MBO) except that they use relative performance targets rather than preset fixed targets.[34] Statoil also has a group bonus scheme and an employee share-purchase scheme.[35]

Borealis have connected bonuses to a scorecard with capped performance targets (as discussed in chapter 5).[36] Initially, the measures were not weighted, but then they selected "golden KPIs" that received higher weights. Some of the problems Borealis has experienced include too much scorecard-based attention on KPIs, with less effort put into strategy development (e.g., strategy maps) and improving the measurement of some KPIs. At Borealis, they also recognize that too much of the focus was on negotiating the level of difficulty for the KPIs. These problems are similar to problems with traditional budgeting systems.

Rather than abolishing budgets, most organizations are being more flexible in their target-setting approaches.

How Are Organizations Changing Their Budgeting Systems?

Organizations still use budgets as an important part of their performance management system, despite all the discussion about problems with budgeting systems. Most organizations are adapting their budgeting systems, rather than abolishing them.[37] Recent research from the United States, Australia, Canada, and Finland suggest that many companies are adapting their budgeting systems by updating budgets more frequently, using subjective performance evaluations, and using rolling forecasts.[38]

One approach is to revise the budget targets more frequently. In the United States, 59% of companies revised the budget targets and of these 27% were at the next budget review, 53% on an ad hoc basis, and 20% were revised when the next rolling budgets were prepared. Similarly, the Canadian survey found that 56% of budgets were revised, and of these, 47% of the revisions occurred at the next budget review, 33% were on an ad hoc basis, and 20% when the next rolling budget was prepared.[39] Survey evidence shows that fewer organizations are using fixed budget targets. A survey of budgeting practices in the United States and Canada has shown that half the companies in the sample were using fixed budgets,[40] and an Australian survey finds that only 34% used annual fixed budgets.[41]

Organizations are using rolling forecasts to adapt to unpredictable environments.[42] A U.S. survey reports that 23% of organizations use rolling budgets, and 62% of these rolling budgets were revised every three months.[43] Similarly, an Australian survey found that 63% of organizations used some type of rolling forecasts. Interestingly, of the Australasian companies that used rolling forecasts, only 3% used rolling forecasts exclusively, whereas 60% used both annual budgets and rolling forecasts.[44] Rolling forecasts are also being used in Finland.[45]

Another common approach is to allow more subjectivity and taking into account other factors (e.g., uncontrollable factors). Some organizations are basing performance evaluations on items within managers' control and then adjusting the budget at the end of the year by actual values using a preagreed formula (we discuss subjective evaluations and controllability issues in chapter 3).[46] Fewer organizations are linking bonuses solely to fixed budgets (9% of firms in the United States and 5% of firms in Canada) and are allowing some subjectivity in performance evaluations for uncontrollable factors instead.[47]

Few companies are implementing the Beyond Budgeting or activity-based budgeting ideas for a number of reasons. It can also be difficult to abolish annual budgets when your external partners require them, as found at Statoil. Another reason is that activity-based budgeting and Beyond Budgeting requires a radical change in the management philosophy. In Borealis, for example, they say they still have balanced scorecards and rolling forecasts but have reverted back to a more traditional management culture brought in by new managers, and so it has gone back on many of the Beyond Budgeting principles.[48]

Summary

Recent innovations in budgeting techniques have been discussed in this chapter. The activity-based budgeting approach focuses on linking operations to the financial plans, a missing link in traditional budgeting systems. Time-driven activity-based budgeting may provide the missing link to operations necessary for a successful balanced scorecard implementation.

In contrast, the Beyond Budgeting advocates argue it is better to abandon budgets and replace them with a completely new management model that focuses on relative performance evaluation with the benefit of hindsight, rolling forecasts for a range of KPIs (not fixed budget targets), empowerment of lower-level employees, and strong leadership. Whether Beyond Budgeting can be successfully implemented appears to depend on senior managers' ability to bring in the new management philosophy.

In practice, organizations are adapting their budgeting systems to make them more flexible by continually updating forecasts and allowing some degree of subjectivity in their performance evaluation processes. What is important is that innovations to target setting occur, be it incrementally or radically. As the quote at the start of the chapter sums up, be ready for failure along the path of innovation. If fear of failure is paramount, then there will be no innovation in the process of target setting or improvements in business performance. Such fear of failure can draw unduly on the science of target setting and ignore the art of balance and harmony.

Key Learning Outcomes

- Time-driven activity-based budgeting is used with the balanced scorecard to link operations with the financial numbers (e.g., resource allocation, capacity).
- The Beyond Budgeting approach is to abolish budgets by focusing on rolling forecasts, evaluating performance using relative targets with the benefit of hindsight and rolling forecasts, and allowing more input from lower-level managers and a change in the leadership style.
- Most organizations seem to be adapting their budgeting systems by making more frequent revisions of budgets, using rolling forecasts together with annual budgets, and allowing some subjectivity in evaluating managers performance to take into account other factors and controllability issues.

CHAPTER 8

Conclusion: Target Setting, the Lost Art

Setting specific targets leads to better performance. Targets encourage employees to find new ways to perform better and allow them to build on prior knowledge. Therefore, specific and challenging targets are better than no targets at all or telling people to *do your best*.[1] How managers deal with multiple and perhaps conflicting targets is important to understand.

Robert Kaplan highlights the example of General Electric (GE). GE uses one financial and seven nonfinancial measures:[2]

1. profitability (residual income)
2. market share
3. productivity
4. product leadership
5. public responsibility
6. personnel development
7. employee attitude
8. balance between short-range and long-range objectives

Targets 5 and 8 clearly capture the importance of ethical behavior as well as value-added activities in the long term. Yet Kaplan notes that senior managers tend to focus on target 1 with the sad tale of several GE units being convicted of price fixing. The pressure of short-term profits made managers trade off targets 8 and 5 to achieve targets 1 and 3. Does this necessarily mean that target setting is inherently flawed?

To answer this question, consider the views of analysts and the stock market. Analysts and stock markets react vigorously to any adjustment downwards to the forecasted quarterly earnings, as the market believes even a small adjustment means that "Not being able to find one or two cents to hit the target might be interpreted as evidence of hidden problems at the firm" or that the firm is poorly managed in the sense that it cannot accurately predict its own future.[3] Organizations must meet their forecasted financial targets. "Show us the money!" Therefore, targets play a key role in an organization's activities.

Financial targets are developed in the budgeting process. Budgets are used for many purposes including coordination, communication, planning, control, and motivation (chapter 2). Operational budgets are short-term plans that need to be integrated with the strategic or long-term plans. However well a budgetary process is designed, it is how the budget is *used* that matters. Therefore, do not blame the budgeting process when managers who are evaluated on their business unit performance fight to maintain their fiefdoms. Given the political arena of negotiating budget targets between managers and head office, clearly the behavioral impacts need to be understood.

Choosing the correct targets is an important part of target setting.[4] Targets need to meet the strategic aspirations of an organization. The strategic planning and thinking processes such as analyzing competitor actions, understanding how to cocreate value with customers, and developing innovations form the basis to challenge and debate options. Empowered employees should be encouraged to seek innovations, set the targets, and test the strategy. Frontline employees know the issues customers are concerned about. Therefore, encourage employees to join with senior management to debate the key issues: Is the organization targeting the right market? Is this target sacred to the organization? Which targets are crucial to success? Who takes responsibility for these performance targets? How often should the targets be reported on, and who should have this information? How is performance to target to be evaluated and who will do the evaluations? Allowing employees to participate in the selection of targets as well as the level of difficulty not only empowers them to take ownership of the targets but also ensures that the customer is not forgotten.

The targets must be relevant at the particular level they are monitored and evaluated. The idea that individuals need to have *line of sight* has been introduced earlier (chapter 1). By having line of sight means that they can see how they can achieve the targets through their actions. This requires targets to be set at lower organizational levels where the individual or team or business unit is being monitored and evaluated. Regularly monitoring performance to targets and providing feedback is also essential. Managers must have control over the resources they need to achieve the targets. This requires a balance between a manager's authority (ability to influence) and his/her responsibility (for what they are accountable).

Organizations use a variety of approaches to strategic planning, capital expenditure planning, and operational budgeting, depending on the context in which they operate (chapter 2). To enable target setting to begin, an analysis of the underlying activities is essential because certain operational activities are strategic necessities and cannot be eliminated. Important questions need to be answered. What are the value drivers of the organization? What are the activities or processes that are essential for the organization to be different from competitors?

The time horizon is also important. Operational budgets are the short-run part of longer-term strategic planning, so it is critical to avoid a short-term focus, allow time for the strategic initiatives to deliver the benefits (e.g., medium-term targets), and track the progress on the strategic initiatives. The reason is that discretionary costs (e.g., marketing for new products and services) can be easily cut or delayed to improve short-term profits, but this can have serious implications on future performance.

Having found the correct targets, is it now a straightforward matter to impose the targets in a top-down manner? If the business seeks empowered employees who drive innovation and best practice, think about taking a bottom-up approach. The various ways that performance targets can be set (e.g., top-down, bottom-up participation, negotiation, ratcheting) are discussed in chapter 4. In establishing targets, more businesses are using relative targets to evaluate performance with internal or external benchmarks. Where external benchmarking is preferred, it should not be done at the cost of losing sight of what key activities help make the organization unique (chapter 4). The answer here is to understand your business by conducting analysis using techniques such as *what if* scenarios and customer profitability analysis. Test this analysis against your gut instinct. Does the analysis (the science) agree with your instincts (the art)? Another good idea is to map out the costs for these activities. Time-driven activity-based budgeting is useful here, and these cost estimates can be used as a basis for target setting. The main advantage of activity-based budgeting is that it links operational activities with the financial numbers and this makes the budgets easier to manage (see chapter 7).

Targets should change as the environmental conditions changes. Target setting is akin to an archer drawing a bow while keeping the arrow true to the target. If there are crosswinds or conditions of environmental uncertainty, the probability of hitting the target is reduced. Many organizations do not seem to vary the target, given the encroaching competitor positions, aging product life cycles or changing customer preferences. Rather, these organizations take the easy option by continually ratcheting up the targets such as sales (grow by 5%) and reducing costs (by 7%) as a way of growing profit by 12%. This begs the question: How do you know that a stretch target (e.g., 5% increase in revenue) is too Olympian? If the industry is facing a shakeout and foreign competitors are entering at a rapid rate, just keeping last year's revenue is a stretch. Trying to squeeze additional growth of 5% in revenues may be unrealistic and stressful for employees. They may resort to gamesmanship or unethical behavior that puts the business reputation at risk.

A better approach is to focus on strategic initiatives such as developing new products or adapting existing products to new markets that can be the source of future growth. In other words, longer term thinking encourages new products and innovative employee practices rather than short-term operational efficiency. After all, Porter warns that operational efficiency is not a strategy.[5] Selecting the best or most critical set of KPIs is better than a simple ratcheting exercise.

The Beyond Budgeting advocates also recommend that the attention should be on tracking performance to rolling forecasts for a few critical key performance indicators (KPIs) (see chapter 7). In fast-growing and rapidly changing industries, more managers use rolling forecasts or regularly revise budget targets to take into account changing conditions (see chapter 3). These rolling forecasts are more accurate as they are continually updated and, therefore, are more useful to predict what is expected to happen in the future. The gap between the performance targets and the rolling forecasts still needs to be the focus of top management attention. Other ways to make targets more flexible are to use subjective evaluations or relative performance evaluations. Therefore a flexible approach to target setting is useful if you have bad forecasts or are unable to make forecasts.

The level of target difficulty depends on the purpose of the target. One purpose is to motivate managers (chapter 5). Olympian targets can be useful to show the future direction of the organization as well as stretch the manager. However, setting Olympian targets for the short term can lead to serious problems because targets are only motivational if people perceive they can be achieved. Difficult targets that are seen as unachievable can lead to job-related tension and reduced performance because of exhaustion and mental fatigue. Increasing target difficulty can also lead to increased stress. The more difficult the target, the better the performance, but this holds only up to the point where the targets are seen as attainable and then performance drops off. The problem is that without the benefit of hindsight, it is difficult to determine the level of target difficulty.

The traditional wisdom was that Olympian targets were necessary to motivate managers. However, in the 1990s, studies found that profit center managers were expected to achieve their targets with a high level of probability, that is, around 80% or 90% of the time.[6] This means that these profit center managers were expected to meet and usually met their budget targets.[7] Having highly achievable targets gives a number of advantages for managers and organizations.

Business unit managers have strong incentives to negotiate highly achievable targets because this influences their evaluations and rewards.[8] A main advantage of highly achievable targets is that this increases managers' line of sight as achievable targets show them how their actions can lead to achieving or beating the performance targets and links budget performance to higher bonuses. Reaching or exceeding budget targets also creates winners, and this is important to boost confidence. In addition, these managers have more operating flexibility to react to short-term events and to take actions such as making preliminary investments in new strategic options without having to get top management's approval. Another advantage is that it reduces the incentive for managers to engage in earnings management (e.g., bringing forward sales, deferring discretionary expenses) and other gaming practices (e.g., false sales) to increase profits. Managers are more likely to invest in longer-term projects.

Top managers also have strong incentives to set highly achievable targets.[9] Overall organizational targets given to analysts, financiers, and other funding bodies will be achieved (and possibly exceeded). This builds up confidence in the market place. The use of highly achievable targets also promotes a stronger commitment from managers to meeting the targets and provides some "cushioning" for uncontrollable events, such as the global financial crisis. Targets that are seen as impossible to achieve do not motivate managers (in fact, they "give up"), and they can also encourage game playing. While targets can be adjusted at the end of the year, organizations are reluctant to do this because it can lead to perceptions of biases, and negotiating the adjustments can take a lot of time. Having highly achievable targets also protects an organization from the impact of over-optimistic estimates of sales, because the higher level of activity that the whole the organization "gears up" to meet never eventuates. A final reason is that highly achievable targets that are linked to bonuses (rather than promotions) mean that employees receive competitive compensation packages, and they are affordable as annual pay varies with profit. Retention of valued employees and competent managers is important.

Allowing managers to negotiate highly achievable targets has some disadvantages. Employees may be paid higher bonuses than they deserve, and managers who wish to maximize their bonuses may still engage in game playing. Setting highly achievable targets may mean that an organization becomes complacent and potentially out-performed by competitors if the focus is not on being best in class. Another problem is that some managers may benefit from good luck or windfall gains rather than their own efforts. For these reasons the Beyond Budgeting advocates argue for performance to be evaluated based on actual performance and compared to peers who had to deal with similar issues (e.g., currency fluctuations, rising oil prices). This is called relative performance evaluation with the benefit of hindsight (chapter 7).

Another option is to reward managers for different levels of performance (e.g., minimum, target, maximum) (chapter 5). The idea is to continue to motivate managers to keep trying to improve performance even when they will not meet the target, or when they have already exceeded the targets. Threshold levels (minimum performance) are set at a level below which no bonuses are paid, and some bonus is provided for managers who have not met their targets. Additional bonuses are also provided for those managers who have exceeded their targets up to a maximum level. The gaming issues around the thresholds and maximum levels are well known and require transactions around balance date to be closely monitored.

The level of target difficulty for the other purposes of target setting, apart from motivation, also needs to be considered. One issue that confronts target setting is that budgets are often used for a range of purposes such as forecasting, evaluation, and resource allocation. Proponents of Beyond Budgeting have argued that using the same budget target for three conflicting purposes "destroys value." They argue that different targets should be used for different purposes. They recommend relative targets be used for performance evaluation. Forecasts need to indicate *expected* performance and this is achieved by regularly updating the rolling forecasts. Separate targets are used for resource allocations that are available when the resources are needed.

Despite the strong criticisms of budget target processes, we caution against throwing the "baby out with the bath water." Budgets require communication and coordination to enable planning, control and evaluation. We agree that resource allocation should not be tied to a yearly cycle. Just as many organizations are updating their budget forecasts more regularly (quarterly or biannually), surely the resource allocation or capital expenditure plans can also be more frequent. Rather than throwing out the budget as advocated by the Beyond Budgeting group (see chapter 5), many companies are revising budget targets more frequently and moving from performance compared to fixed targets to taking into account other factors such as uncontrollable events and allowing more subjectivity. The over reliance of traditional fixed budget targets used for a myriad of conflicting purposes (e.g. evaluation, planning, control and resource allocation) highlights the dangers of relying too much on financial targets as measures of performance.

To overcome the limitations of focusing on a single target, the focus should be on a few critical targets that include a mix of financial and nonfinancial measures (chapter 6). Using multiple performance measures reduces the opportunity for gaming and unethical behavior. Having multiple performance targets requires a balance between the objective and subjective uses of measures for performance evaluation. The use of multiple performance measures means that they provide information on different aspects of performance that is often not available or lost when information is aggregated.

While multiple performance measures are useful, meeting quarterly profit forecasts results in a great deal of pressure. Financial performance is critical, with the mantra being, "Show me the money." This raises an interesting question that if a given profitability is achieved, does this mean that value is still not lost? Not so, a stable earnings per share (EPS) may still mask that long-term value is being lost. A recent study found that Chief Financial Officers (CFOs) sacrificed value to smooth earnings.[10] This sacrifice in value occurred by not investing in new projects, research and development, repairs and maintenance, and other discretionary expenditures. Why do some executives sacrifice value to achieve a target of smooth earnings? This was not merely creative accounting as these CFOs understood that after the Sarbanes-Oxley Legislation in the United States, such manipulations would easily be second guessed by auditors and frowned on by the board of directors. Rather, these CFOs just did not spend the money as the likely returns were longer than the short-term reporting period. Why? As one CFO stated, volatile earnings would cost them their job or raise the ire of the stock market.[11]

The focus needs to be on the few critical targets that are pivotal to the strategic growth of the business. Thinking about the weighting of the targets is important. However, in using multiple targets, are some of the targets substitutes? In other words, some targets capture aspects of performance similar to other targets, but some do not. Avoid the easy option of comparing performance to targets for everything that can be counted. Not everything that can be counted or measured is important. The rise of enterprise resource planning systems or corporate software means that thousands of measures can be extracted on a daily, monthly, or quarterly basis. The sheer volume of numbers, ratios, operational indicators, and customer measures can overwhelm the busy executive. To simplify the quantum of numbers is essential. Two hundred lines of a budget undergoing variance analysis is just time consuming and does not improve decision making. Additional measures and targets should be used if they provide additional information on performance. Managers have more discretion over certain budgetary targets, such as research and development, repairs and maintenance, or marketing expenditure to develop a line of brands, than operational items. These financial targets should be linked to nonfinancial targets. For example, in the airline industry, cutting back on repairs and maintenance to beat the budget target is strategic suicide. This highlights how some performance targets can be destructive. Rather, performance should be tracked to nonfinancial targets, such as number of hours of maintenance or types of testing for various components. For service-oriented businesses, the dollar value in the budget (or percentage of sales revenue locked in for training) is a financial measure. This financial measure must be committed, and the important nonfinancial targets will include the number of hours or days for training employees, and developing and measuring key competencies. These nonfinancial targets are mapped to the new range of services, products, or new niche of clients to be attracted to the business. This is the principle of the strategy map used in the balanced scorecard (chapter 6).

This book highlights the complex nature of target setting in organizations. Getting target setting "right" is not just a matter of imposing targets in a top-down manner! Not surprisingly, setting performance targets is often described by managers as *"more of an art than a science."*[12] The choices you make in setting targets have important implications for performance management in your organization.

Appendix

Understanding Probabilities

Pillai Company has recently gone through a strategic planning session for all its sales personnel. Based on past experience, the following information is available about sales:

Mean sales for last 5 years	100,000 units
Standard deviation of sales	8,000 units
Last year's sales	106,000 units
Target for next year (5% increase)	111,300 units
Price	$10.00/ unit
Variable costs	$4.80 /unit
Fixed costs	$450,000

Given this information, we will talk our way through targets and probability. For those with an engineering and mathematical background, this section will use means, standard deviation, and the use of z tables. Let us look at a few issues:

1. What is the probability of at least breaking even?
2. What is the probability of achieving next year's sales goal?
3. What additional information do you want to be more confident about your probability assessments in the previous two questions?
4. How would your answer for questions 1 and 2 differ if the mean shifted from 100,000 to 106,000?

Let us answer these questions.

1. What is the probability of at least breaking even?

$$\text{Break Even} = \frac{\text{Fixed Costs}}{\text{Contribution Margin per Unit (selling price less variable costs)}}$$

$$= \frac{\$450,000}{(\$10.00 - \$4.80)}$$

$$= 86,538 \text{ units}$$

The answer is that any number of units above 86, 538 (the break-even point) would be profitable for Pillai Company.

Now, let us use this break-even cost information to work out the probability of breaking even.

$$z = \frac{86,538 - 100,000}{8,000}$$

$$= -1.6826$$

- infinity to -Z

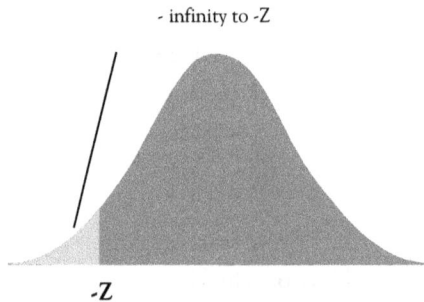

-Z

Take a look at the z Table at the end of this appendix. The arrow pointing to the left hand side of normal distribution shown earlier gives us the answer. Note that a negative z means this value is below the mean. Looking at the z Table at the line with 1.6 and along column .08, we get a value of 0.45352. Now add on the 0.5 of the right tail, and this gives us the overall probability. The answer is 0.95352. This means that we have a 95% probability of breaking even, resulting in little pressure on the manager to break even.

2. What is the probability of achieving next year's sales goal?

Target	111,300 units
Mean	100,000 units
Standard deviation	8,000 units

$$z = \frac{111,300 - 100,000}{8,000}$$

$$z = 1.4125$$

See the next z Table and look along the line with 1.4 and column .01 that has a circle around it.

As z is positive, it is on the right-hand side of the curve.

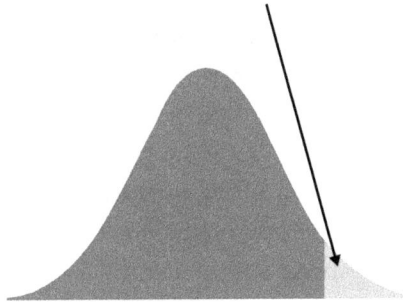

If 0.5 is the right tail, then 0.5 – 0.42073. The answer is 0.08. This means that the manager has an 8% chance of achieving the target. This is quite a stretch target: If the manager does not achieve this business unit performance, what are the consequences?

3. What additional information do you want to be more confident about your probability assessments in the previous two questions?

a. *How useful is the past for predicting the probability of the future?* To address this point, a few issues need to be considered. First, if there is no change in technology, learning by employees, or substantive changes in business processes, the probability assessment is fairly robust. Second, using the past data is valid as it provides a useful range of points to plan and map out. Ignoring the past and forecasting does not give any indication of how robust or confident the estimation of probability is going to be.

b. *Are last year's sales being higher than the mean an indication of changing conditions?* This is the key to setting targets. If this year's sales are higher as the demand for products or services has grown, then clearly the demand function has shifted. However, last year's sales being higher than average does not mean a shift in demand. As you look at a normal curve, last year's sales of 106,000 units was just another point on the distribution. There has been no shift in demand.

c. *What is the distribution of the fixed costs?* Over the points of the normal curve, fixed costs should remain constant. In other words, the costs of capacity or fixed costs should not have changed across the distribution curve. If the fixed costs do change, then it is likely that there is a step function to these costs. In other words, if moving to a sales volume of 106,000 units meant leasing new warehouse space or new machines to manufacture this new capacity, then the cost analysis needs to be investigated further to understand the probability of breaking even.

If the distribution of fixed costs does not change, in other words, across the normal curve for sales, fixed costs remain constant, and the variable cost per unit remains constant (there are no economies or diseconomies of scale), the fundamental cost structure of doing business remains the same across the new level of 106,000 units.

4. How would your answer for questions 1 and 2 differ if the mean shifted from 100,000 to 106,000?

Now we are stating that last year' sales of 106,000 has become the new mean. In other words, we have shifted the curve to the right to get the 106,000 as the peak, resulting in a 50% chance of getting last year's sales as the future target.

Basically, a senior management has decided to increase (or ratchet) the sales forecast where 106,000 units are held to have a 50% likelihood of occurring. They will use the same analysis as the first two questions.

Computing Probability:

$$\frac{86,538 - 106,000}{8,000}$$

$$z = 2.43$$

The probability is 0.49245. This means that the likelihood of achieving the break-even point is now higher and goes to 99.245% (.50 + 0.49245). Increasing performance targets can result in what is called ratcheting and is discussed in chapter 4.

Z Table

This is the area under the normal curve between the mean and successive values of z.

z	.00	.01	.02	.03	.04	.05	.06	.07	.08	.09
.0	.00000	.00399	.00798	.01197	.01595	.01994	.02392	.02790	.03188	.03586
.1	.03983	.04380	.04776	.05172	.05567	.05962	.06356	.06749	.07142	.07535
.2	.07926	.08317	.08706	.09095	.09483	.09871	.10257	.10642	.11026	.11409
.3	.11791	.12172	.12552	.12930	.13307	.13683	.14058	.14431	.14803	.15173
.4	.15542	.15910	.16276	.16640	.17003	.17364	.17724	.18082	.18439	.18793
.5	.19146	.19467	.19847	.20194	.20540	.20884	.21226	.21566	.21904	.22240
.6	.22575	.22907	.23237	.23565	.23891	.24215	.24537	.24857	.25175	.25490
.7	.25804	.26115	.26424	.26730	.27035	.27337	.27637	.27935	.28230	.28524
.8	.28814	.29103	.29389	.29673	.29955	.30234	.30511	.30785	.31057	.31327
.9	.31594	.31859	.32121	.32381	.32639	.32894	.33147	.33398	.33646	.33891
1.0	.34134	.34375	.34614	.34849	.35083	.35314	.35543	.35769	.35993	.36214
1.1	.36433	.36650	.36864	.37076	.37286	.37493	.37698	.37900	.38100	.38298
1.2	.38493	.38686	.38877	.39065	.39251	.39435	.39617	.39796	.39973	.40147
1.3	.40320	.40490	.40658	.40824	.40988	.41149	.41309	.41466	.41621	.41774
1.4	.41924	(.42073)	.42220	.42364	.42507	.42647	.42785	.42922	.43056	.43189
1.5	.43319	.43448	.43574	.43699	.43822	.43943	.44062	.44179	.44295	.44408

z	.00	.01	.02	.03	.04	.05	.06	.07	.08	.09
1.6	.44520	.44630	.44738	.44845	.44950	.45053	.45154	.45254	.45352	.45449
1.7	.45543	.45637	.45728	.45818	.45907	.45994	.46080	.46164	.46246	.46327
1.8	.46407	.46485	.46562	.46638	.46712	.46784	.46856	.46926	.46995	.47062
1.9	.47128	.47193	.47257	.47320	.47381	.47441	.47500	.47558	.47615	.47670
2.0	.47725	.47778	.47831	.47882	.47932	.47982	.48030	.48077	.48124	.48169
2.1	.48214	.48257	.48300	.48341	.48382	.48422	.48461	.48500	.48537	.48574
2.2	.48610	.48645	.48679	.48713	.48745	.48778	.48809	.48840	.48870	.48899
2.3	.48928	.48956	.48983	.49010	.49036	.49061	.49086	.49111	.49134	.49158
2.4	.49180	.49202	.49224	.49245	.49266	.49286	.49305	.49324	.49343	.49361
2.5	.49379	.49396	.49413	.49430	.49446	.49461	.49477	.49492	.49506	.49520
2.6	.49534	.49547	.49560	.49573	.49585	.49598	.49609	.49621	.49632	.49643
2.7	.49653	.49664	.49674	.49683	.49693	.49702	.49711	.49720	.49728	.49736
2.8	.49744	.49752	.49760	.49767	.49774	.49781	.49788	.49795	.49801	.49807
2.9	.49813	.49819	.49825	.49831	.49836	.49841	.49846	.49851	.49856	.49861
3.0	.49865									
4.0	.49997									

Notes

Chapter 1

1. This statement is often used. See for example, Merchant and Van der Stede (2007), p. 477; Stringer (2006), p. 149, p. 354 (italics added).
2. Dishneau (1992).
3. Simons (1995a); Simons (1995b).
4. See Vroom (1964); Heneman and Gresham (2002).
5. Heneman and Gresham (2002), p. 90.
6. See Heneman and Gresham (2002); Lawler (2000); Vroom (1964).
7. Ferreira and Otley (2009).
8. Stringer (2007); Kaplan (2006b).

Chapter 2

1. EVA® is the registered trademark of Stern Stewart (http://www.eva.com/).
2. Hansen et al. (2003).
3. Hansen et al. (2003).
4. Sivabalan et al. (2009).
5. Kaplan (2010).
6. Libby and Lindsay (2010).
7. Blumentritt (2006).
8. Merchant and Van der Stede (2007).
9. Hamel and Prahalad (1993).
10. Hamel and Prahalad (1993).
11. Merchant (2006).
12. See Dye and Sibony (2007).
13. Argyris (1952).
14. Taylor (1916).
15. Hopwood (1972).
16. The name Astoria has been given to ensure confidentiality of the organization.
17. Frow et al. (2009); Marginson et al. (2006).
18. Frow et al. (2009).

Chapter 3

1. Adapted from Heitger et al. (1992).
2. Merchant and Van der Stede (2007).
3. Merchant and Van der Stede (2007).
4. See Hope and Frazer (2003); Morlidge and Player (2010).
5. Merchant and Van der Stede (2007).
6. Gibbs et al. (2004).
7. See Ahrens and Chapman (2002); Merchant et al. (2010).
8. Hopwood (1972).
9. Indjejikian (1999).
10. Libby and Lindsay (2010); Merchant (1990).
11. Stringer (2006).
12. Otley (1999); Merchant and Van der Stede (2007).
13. Merchant (1989).
14. Heneman et al. (2002).
15. Baker et al. (1988).
16. Libby and Lindsay (2007, 2010).
17. Libby and Lindsay (2010).
18. Bol (2008).
19. Jensen et al. (2004).
20. Merchant (2009).
21. Merchant and Van der Stede (2007).
22. Bol (2008); Merchant et al. (2010).
23. Gibbs et al. (2005).
24. Gibbs et al. (2004).
25. Gibbs et al. (2004).
26. Merchant et al. (2010).
27. Konovsky et al. (1992).

Chapter 4

1. Murphy (2001).
2. Murphy (2001).
3. Towers Perrin's *Annual Incentive Plan Design Survey* in 1997 shows internal standards are commonly used in incentive plans, with only 11% of companies surveyed using external standards (Murphy, 2001).
4. These are discussed in most papers on benchmarking, including Elmuti and Kathawala (1997).
5. Northcott and Llewellyn (2003).
6. Kaplan (2005).
7. Hansen et al. (2003).

8. Matsumura and Yong Shin (2006).

9. Matsumura and Yong Shin (2006).

10. Merchant and Van der Stede (2007).

11. Libby and Lindsay (2010).

12. Argyris (1952).

13. Schiff and Lewin (1970).

14. Merchant and Van der Stede (2007).

15. Leone and Rock (2002).

16. Matsumura and Yong Shin (2006).

17. Zimmerman (2006).

18. Leone and Rock (2002).

19. Indejikian and Nanda (2002).

20. Mortidge and Player (2010) provides a good overview of forecasting for performance targets.

21. Zimmerman (2006).

22. Neely et al. (2001).

23. Hackett Group (2008).

24. Collier and Berry (2002).

25. Anthony and Govindarajan (2007).

26. The origins of zero-based budgeting can be traced to the late 1900s. See Burrows and Syme (2000).

27. Zimmerman (2006).

28. Neely et al. (2001).

Chapter 5

1. Merchant and Van der Stede (2007).

2. Locke and Latham (1990, 2006).

3. There are different definitions of a stretch target; sometimes it refers to Olympian targets (Kerr and Landaur, 2004).

4. Merchant and Manzoni (1989); Gibbs et al. (2004); Merchant and Otley (2007).

5. Stringer (2006).

6. Locke and Latham (1990, 2006).

7. Latham and Baldes (1975).

8. Latham and Baldes (1975).

9. Locke and Latham (2002); Latham and Baldes (1975).

10. Locke and Latham (2002).

11. Taylor (1916).

12. Taylor (1916), pp. 48–49.

13. While the core principles of goal-setting theory at the individual level have been well supported, goal-setting studies have primarily been based on

experiments with nonmanagers (often student surrogates) doing simple tasks (Locke & Latham, 1990).

14. Locke and Latham (2006, 2002).

15. Ordonez et al. (2009).

16. Schweitzer et al. (2004).

17. Kerr and Landauer (2004).

18. Chan (1998).

19. Hopwood (1974).

20. Yerkes-Dodson Law, see Yerkes and Dodson (1908).

21. Campbell and Furrer (1995); Onyemah (2008).

22. Libby and Lindsay (2010).

23. Merchant and Van der Stede (2007).

24. Merchant and Manzoni (1989).

25. Merchant (1990); Merchant and Manzoni (1989).

26. Adapted from Merchant and Otley (2007); Jensen (2001).

27. Merchant and Manzoni (1989).

28. Jensen et al. (2004).

29. Data from the Towers Perrin Annual Incentive Plan Survey in 1997 (cited in Murphy, 2001).

30. Jensen (2001).

31. Libby and Lindsay (2010).

32. Merchant and Van der Stede (2007).

33. Watson Wyatt Worldwide, *Executive pay in 2002: Compensation in turbulent times,* (2001/2002 survey report, p. 12), cited in Merchant and Van der Stede (2007).

34. Walsh (2000).

35. Merchant (1990).

36. Merchant et al. (2010).

37. Merchant and Van der Stede (2007).

38. Haka and Krishnan (2005).

Chapter 6

1. Merchant (2006).

2. Hansen (2010); Ittner and Larcker (2003); Kaplan and Norton (2008); Otley (1999).

3. Ittner and Larcker (2003).

4. Ittner and Larcker (2003).

5. Cohan (2002).

6. Ittner et al. (2003); Lipe and Salterio (2000).

7. Luft and Shields (2001); Schiff and Hoffman (1996).

8. Merchant (2006).

9. Kaplan and Norton (2008).

10. Merchant and Van der Stede (2007), p. 477.

11. Stringer (2006).

12. Ittner and Larcker (2003).

13. Kaplan and Norton (2008).

14. Ittner and Larcker (2003).

15. Ittner and Larcker (2003).

16. See Ahrens and Chapman (2002); Merchant and Riccaboni (1990); Otley (1990).

17. Ittner and Larcker (2003).

18. Ittner et al. (1997).

19. Ittner and Larcker (2003).

20. Ittner and Larcker (2003).

21. Ittner and Larcker (2003).

22. Merchant (2006).

23. Merchant (2006).

24. Stringer (2006).

25. Merchant (2006); Anthony and Govindarajan (2007).

26. Ittner and Larcker (2003).

27. Ittner et al. (2003).

28. Merchant (2006).

29. For example, Banker and Datar (1989); Feltham and Xie (1994).

30. Kerr (1975).

31. Ittner and Larcker (2003).

32. This example was conducted as part of an MBA research project.

33. Merchant and Van der Stede (2007).

34. Merchant (2009).

Chapter 7

1. Adapted from Neely et al. (2001), p. 6–7.

2. Kaplan and Atkinson (1998).

3. Kaplan and Anderson (2004).

4. Kaplan and Anderson (2004).

5. Kaplan and Norton (2008).

6. Cooper and Kaplan (1998).

7. Kaplan and Anderson (2007). For the Sippican case study, see R. S. Kaplan, "Sippican Corporation (A), Case 9-106-060 (Boston: Harvard Business School, 2006).

8. Adapted from Brimson and Antos (1999).

9. Stratton (2006).

10. Hansen et al. (2003)

11. Hope and Fraser (2003a). The Beyond Budgeting Roundtable website is available at http://www/bbrt.org

12. Bogsnes (2007).

13. Lindsay and Libby (2007).

14. Hope and Fraser (2003a).

15. Morlidge and Player (2010); Bogsnes (2007).

16. Bogsnes (2007).

17. Bogsnes (2007).

18. Bogsnes (2007).

19. Hope and Fraser (2003b).

20. Bogsnes (2007).

21. Hope and Fraser (2003b).

22. Bogsnes (2007).

23. Statoil (2010).

24. Merchant and Van der Stede (2011).

25. Merchant and Van der Stede (2011).

26. Merchant and Van der Stede (2011).

27. Bogsnes (2007).

28. Merchant and Van der Stede (2011), p. 5, footnote 5.

29. Merchant and Van der Stede (2011), p. 5, footnote 5.

30. Hansen et al. (2003).

31. Hope and Fraser (2003a).

32. Matsumura and Yong Shin (2006).

33. Carter et al. (2009).

34. Bogsnes (2007).

35. Bogsnes (2007).

36. Bogsnes (2007).

37. Ekholm and Wallin (2000).

38. Ekholm and Wallin (2000).

39. Libby and Lindsay (2010).

40. Libby and Lindsay (2010).

41. Sivabalan et al. (2009).

42. Libby and Lindsay (2010).

43. Hansen and Van der Stede (2004).

44. Sivabalan et al. (2009).

45. Ekholm and Wallin (2000).

46. Libby and Lindsay (2010).

47. Libby and Lindsay (2010).

48. Bogsnes (2007).

Chapter 8

1. Locke and Latham (1990, 2006).

2. Kaplan (2010).

3. Graham et al. (2006).

4. Merchant and Manzoni (1989).

5. Porter (1996).

6. Merchant and Manzoni (1989); Merchant (1990).

7. Merchant and Manzoni (1989).

8. Merchant and Manzoni (1989); Merchant (1990).

9. Merchant and Manzoni (1989); Merchant (1990).

10. Graham et al. (2006).

11. Graham et al. (2006).

12. Adapted from Merchant and Van der Stede (2007, p. 477) and Stringer (2006, p. 149, p. 354). Italics added.

References

Ahrens, T., & Chapman, C. (2002). The structuration of legitimate performance measures and management: Day-to-day contests of accountability in a UK restaurant chain. *Management Accounting Research, 13*, 151–171.

Anthony, R., & Govindarajan, V. (2007). *Management control systems* (12th ed.). Singapore: Irwin.

Argyris, C. (1952). *The Impact of budgets on people.* New York, NY: Controllership Foundation.

Ariely, D., Gneezy, U., Loewenstein, G., & Mazar, N. (2009). Large stakes and big mistakes. *Review of Economic Studies, 76*(2), 451–469.

Baker, G. P., Jensen, M. C., & Murphy, K. J. (1988). Compensation and incentives: Practice vs. theory. *The Journal of Finance, 43*(3), 593–616.

Banker, R. D., and Datar, S. M. (1989, Spring). Sensitivity, precision, and linear aggregation of signals for performance evaluation. *Journal of Accounting Research, 27*(1), 21–39.

Blumentritt, T. (2006). Integrating strategic management and budgeting. *Journal of Business Strategy, 27*(6), 73–79.

Bogsnes B. (2007). *Implementing beyond budgeting: Unlocking the performance potential.* Hoboken, NJ: Wiley.

Bol, J. C. (2008). Subjectivity in compensation contracting. *Journal of Accounting Literature, 27*, 1–32.

Brimson, J. A., & Antos, J. (1999). *Driving value using activity-based budgeting.* Wiley Cost Management Series. New York: Wiley.

Burrows, G., & Syme, B. (2000). Zero-based budgeting: Origins and pioneers. *ABACUS, 36*(2), 226–241.

Campbell, D. J., & Furrer, D. M. (1995). Goal setting and competition as determinants of task performance. *Journal of Organizational Behavior, 16*(4), 377–389.

Carter M., Ittner, C., & Zechman, S. (2009). Explicit relative performance evaluation in performance-vested equity grants. *Review of Accounting Studies, 14*(2/3), 269–306. doi:10.1007/s11142-009-9085-8

Chan, C. W. (1998). Transfer pricing negotiation outcomes and the impact of negotiator mixed-motives and culture: Empirical evidence from the U.S. and Australia. *Management Accounting Research, 9*(2), 139–161.

Cohan, J. A. (2002). "I didn't know" and "I was only doing my job": Has corporate governance careened out of control? A case study of Enron's information myopia. *Journal of Business Ethics, 30*(3), 275–299.

Collier, P. M., & Berry, A. J. (2002). Risk in the process of budgeting. *Management Accounting Research*, *13*(3), 273–297.

Cooper, R., & Kaplan, R. S. (1998, July–August). The promise—and peril—of integrated cost systems (HBR 98403). *Harvard Business Review*, *76*(4), 109–119.

Dishneau, D. (1992, June 22). Sears admits mistakes, takes workers off commission. The Associated Press.

Dye, R., & Sibony, O. (2007, August). How to improve strategic planning. *McKinsey Quarterly*, *3*, 40–49. Retrieved from http://www.mckinseyquarterly.com/Strategy/Strategy_in_Practice/How_to_improve_strategic_planning_2026

Ekholm, B.-G., & Wallin, J. (2001). Is the annual budget really dead? *The European Accounting Review*, *9*(4), 519–539. doi:10.1080/09638180020024007

Elmuti, D., & Kathawala, Y. (1997). An overview of benchmarking process: A tool for continuous improvement and competitive advantage. *Benchmarking for Quality Management & Technology*, *4*(4), 249–243.

Feltham, G. A. & Xie, J. (1994, July). Performance measure congruity and diversity in multi-task principal/agent relations. *Accounting Review*, *69*(3), 429–453.

Ferreira, A. & Otley, D. (2009). The design and use of performance management systems: An extended framework for analysis. *Management Accounting Research*, *20*(4), 263–282.

Folger, R., Konovsky, M. A., & Cropazo, R. (1992). A due process metaphor for performance appraisal. *Research in Organizational Behavior*, *14*, 129–177.

Frow, N., Marginson, D., & Ogden, S. (2009). "Continuous" budgeting: Reconciling budget flexibility. *Accounting Organisations & Society*, *35*(4), p. 444–461.

Gibbs, M., Merchant, K. A., Van der Stede, W. A., & Vargas, M. E. (2004). Determinants and effects of subjectivity in incentives. *The Accounting Review*, *79*(2), 409–436.

Gibbs, M., Merchant, K. A., Van der Stede, W., & Vargus, M. E. (2005, May/June). The benefits of evaluating performance subjectively. *Performance Improvement*, *44*(5), 26–32.

Graham, J. R., Harvey, C. R., & Rajgopal, S. (2006, November–December). Value destruction and financial reporting decisions. *Financial Analysts Journal*, *62*(6), 27–39.

Hackett Group. (2008) Hackett: Despite prospect of harsh punishment by Wall Street, most companies fail when forecasting earnings and sales. Press release. Retrieved from http://www.thehackettgroup.com/about/alerts/alerts_2008/alert_02122008.jsp

Haka, S., & Krishnan, R. (2005). Budget type and performance—The moderating effect of uncertainty. *Australian Accounting Review, 15*(1), 3–13.

Hamel, G., & Prahalad, C. K. (1993, March–April). Strategy as stretch and leverage. *Harvard Business Review, 71*(2), 75–84.

Hansen, A. (2010). Nonfinancial measures, externalities and target setting: A comparative case study of resolutions through planning. *Management Accounting Research, 21*(1), 17–39.

Hansen, S. C., & Van der Stede, W. A. (2004). Multiple facets of budgeting: An exploratory analysis. *Management Accounting Research, 15*(4), 415–439.

Hansen, S. C., Otley, D. T., & Van de Stede, W. A. (2003). Practice developments in budgeting: An overview and research perspective. *Journal of Management Accounting Research, 15*, 95–116.

Heitger, L., Ogan, P., & Matulich S. (1992). *Cost accounting* (2nd ed.). Cincinnati, OH: South-Western Publishing.

Heneman, R. L., & Gresham, M. T. (2002). Performance-based pay plans. In R. L. Heneman (Ed.), *Strategic reward management: Design, implementation, and evaluation* (pp. 75–109). Greenwich, CT: Information Age Publishing.

Heneman, R. L., Ledford, G. E., Jr., & Gresham, M. T. (2002). The changing nature of work and its effects on compensation design and delivery. In R. L. Heneman (Ed.), *Strategic reward management: Design, implementation, and evaluation* (pp. 35–73). Greenwich, CT: Information Age Publishing.

Hope, J., & Fraser, R. (2003a). *Beyond budgeting: How managers can break free of the annual performance trap.* Cambridge, MA: Harvard Business School Press.

Hope, J., & Fraser, R. (2003b, Feb.). Who Needs Budgets? *Harvard Business Review, 81*(2) 108–115.

Hopwood, A. G. (1972). An empirical study of the role of accounting data in performance evaluation. *Journal of Accounting Research*, supplement, *10*(3), 156–182.

Hopwood, A. G. (1974). *Accounting and human behaviour.* Englewood Cliffs, NJ: Prentice-Hall.

Indjejikian, R. J. (1999). Performance evaluation and compensation research: An agency perspective. *Accounting Horizons, 13*(2), 147–157.

Indjejikian, R. J., & Nanda, D. J. (2002). Executive target bonuses and what they imply about performance standards. *The Accounting Review, 77*(4), 793–819.

Ittner, C. D., & Larcker, D. F. (2003, November). Coming up short on nonfinancial performance measurement. *Harvard Business Review, 81*(11), 88–95.

Ittner, C. D., Larcker, D. F., & Meyer, M. W. (2003). Subjectivity and the weighting of performance measures: Evidence from a balanced scorecard. *The Accounting Review, 78*(3), 725–728.

Ittner, C. D., Larcker, D. F., & Rajan, M. V. (1997). The choice of performance measures in annual bonus contracts. *The Accounting Review, 72*(2), 231–255.

Jensen, M. (2001). Corporate budgeting is broken—Let's fix it. *Harvard Business Review, 70*(10), 95–101.

Jensen, M. C., Murphy, K. J., & Wruck, E. G. (2004). *Remuneration: Where we've been, how we got to here, what are the problems, and how to fix them.* European Corporate Governance Institute, Finance Working Paper no. 44. Retrieved from: http://papers.ssrn.com/sol3/papers.cfm?abstract_id=561305

Kaplan, R. S. (2005, November–December). The limits of benchmarking, balanced scorecard report. *Harvard Business Review.* Reprint #B0511C. Retrieved from http://hbr.org/product/limits-of-benchmarking/an/B0511C -HCB-ENG

Kaplan, R. S. (2006a). Sippican Corporation (A), Case 9-106-060. Boston: Harvard Business School Press. Retrieved from http://hbr.org/product/sippican -corp-a/an/106058-PDF-ENG

Kaplan, R. S. (2006b). Target setting, Balanced Scorecard Report, Harvard Business School Publishing, article reprint no. B0605C. Retrieved from http:// hbr.org/product/target-setting/an/B0605C-PDF-ENG

Kaplan, R. S. (2010). Conceptual foundations of the balanced scorecard. Harvard Business School, Working Paper 10–074. Retrieved from http://hbswk .hbs.edu/item/6395.html

Kaplan, R. S., & Anderson, S. R. (2004, November). Time-driven activity-based costing. *Harvard Business Review, 82*(11), 131–138.

Kaplan, R. S., & Anderson, S. R. (2007). *Time-driven activity-based costing: A simpler and more powerful path to higher profits.* Boston: Harvard Business School Press.

Kaplan, R. S., & Atkinson, A. A. (1998). *Advanced management accounting* (3rd ed.). Upper Saddle River, NJ: Prentice-Hall.

Kaplan, R. S., & Norton, D. P. (2008, January). Mastering the management system. Special Issue on HBS Centennial. *Harvard Business Review, 86*(1), 62–77.

Kerr, S. (1975). On the folly of rewarding A, while hoping for B. *The Academy of Management Journal, 18*(4), 769–783.

Latham, G. P., & Baldes, J. (1975). The "practical significance" of Locke's theory of goal setting. *Journal of Applied Psychology, 60*(1), 122–124.

Lawler, E. E., III. (2000). *Rewarding excellence, pay strategies for the new economy.* San Francisco, CA: Jossey-Bass.

Leone, A. J., & Rock, S. (2002). Empirical tests of budget ratcheting and its effect on managers' discretionary accrual choices. *Accounting and Economics, 33,* 43–67.

Libby, T., & Lindsay, R., M. (2007, August). Beyond budgeting or better budgeting? *Strategic Finance Journal, 89*(2) 47–51.

Libby, T., & Lindsay, R. M. (2010). Beyond budgeting or budgeting reconsidered? A survey of North-American budgeting practice. *Management Accounting Research*, *21*(1), 56–75.

Lindsay, R. M., & Libby, T. (2007, November). Svenska Handelsbanken: Controlling a radically decentralized organization without budgets. *Issues in Accounting Education*, *22*(4), 625–640.

Lipe, M. G., & Salterio, S. E. (2000). The balanced scorecard: Judgmental effects of common and unique performance measures. *The Accounting Review*, *75*(3), 283–298.

Locke, E. A., & Latham, G. P. (1990). *The theory of goal setting and task performance*. Englewood Cliffs, NJ: Prentice-Hall.

Locke, E. A., & Latham, G. P. (2002). Building a practically useful theory of goal setting and task motivation: A 35-year odyssey. *American Psychologist*, *57*(9), 705–717.

Locke, E. A., & Latham, G. P. (2006). New directions in goal setting theory. *Association for Psychological Sciences*, *15*(5), 265–268.

Luft, J. L., & Shields, M. D. (2001). Why does fixation persist? Experimental evidence on the judgment performance effects of expensing intangibles. *The Accounting Review*, *76*(4), 561–587.

Marginson, D., Ogden, S., & Frow, N. (2006). *Budgeting and innovation. Complements or contradictions?* London, England: CIMA.

Matsumura, E. M., & Shin, J. Y. (2006). An empirical analysis of an incentive plan with relative performance measures: Evidence from a postal service. *The Accounting Review*, *81*(3), 533–566.

Merchant, K.A. (1989) *Rewarding results: motivating profit centre managers*, Harvard Business School Press, Boston.

Merchant, K. A. (1990). The effects of financial controls on data manipulation and management myopia. *Accounting Organisations & Society*, *15*(4), 297–313.

Merchant, K. A. (1998). *Modern management control systems, text and cases*. Englewood Cliffs, NJ: Prentice-Hall.

Merchant, K. A. (2006). Measuring general managers' performances, market, accounting and combination-of-measures systems. *Accounting, Auditing & Accountability Journal*, *19*(6), 893–917.

Merchant, K. A. (2009). The merits and demerits of accounting measures of performance. Plenary Lecture, Performance Measurement Association Conference, University of Otago, Dunedin.

Merchant, K. A., & Manzoni, J. (1989). The achievability of budget targets in profit centres: A field study. *The Accounting Review*, *64*(3), 539–558.

Merchant, K. A., & Otley, D. T. (2007). A review of the literature on control and accountability. In C. S. Chapman, A. G. Hopwood, and M. D. Shields

(Eds.), *Handbook of management accounting research* (Volume 2, pp. 785–804). Oxford: Elsevier.

Merchant, K. A., & Riccaboni, A. (1990). Performance-based management incentives at the Fiat Group: A field study. *Management Accounting Research, 1*(4), 281–303.

Merchant, K. A., Stringer, C. P., & Theivananthampillai, P. (2010, August 2). Relationship between objective and subjective performance measures. Paper presented at the American Accounting Association Conference. Retrieved from: http://aaahq.org/AM2010/concurrent01.cfm

Merchant, K. A., & Van der Stede, W. A. (2007). *Management control systems, performance measurement, evaluation and incentives* (2nd ed.). London, England: Prentice-Hall.

Merchant, K. A., & Van der Stede, W. A. (2011). *Statoil.* London School of Economics and University of Southern California, teaching case (A211–01).

Morlidge, S., & Player, S. (2010). *Future ready: How to master business forecasting.* London, England: Wiley.

Murphy, K. J. (2001). Performance standards in incentive contracts. *Journal of Accounting and Economics, 30,* 245–278.

Neely, A, Sutcliff, M. R., & Heynes, H. R. (2001). *Driving value through strategic planning and budgeting.* New York, NY: Accenture.

Northcott, D., & Llewellyn, S. (2003). The "ladder of success" in healthcare: The UK national reference costing index. *Management Accounting Research, 14*(1), 51–66. doi:10.1016/S1044-5005(02)00032-X

Onyemah, V. (2008, Summer). Role ambiguity, role conflict, and performance: Empirical evidence of an inverted-U relationship. *Journal of Personal Selling & Sales Management, 28*(3), 299–313.

Ordonez, L. D., Schweitzer, M. E., Galinsky, A. D., & Bazerman, M. (2009, February). Goals gone wild: The systematic side effects of overprescribing goal setting. *Academy of Management Perspectives, 23*(1), 6–16.

Otley, D. (1990). Issues in accountability and control: some observations from a study of colliery accountability in the British Coal Corporation. *Management Accounting Research, 1*(2), 101–123.

Otley, D. (1999). Performance management: a framework for management control systems research. *Management Accounting Research, 10*(4), 363–382.

Porter, M. E. (1996, November). What is strategy? *Harvard Business Review, 74*(6) 61–78.

Schiff, A. D., & Hoffman, L. R. (1996). An exploration of the use of financial and nonfinancial measures of performance by executives in a service firm. *Behavioral Research in Accounting, 8*(1), 134–151.

Schiff, W., & Lewin, A. Y. (1970). The impact of people on budgets. *The Accounting Review, 45*(2), 259–268.

Schweitzer, M. E., Ordóñez, L., & Douma, B. (2004). Goal setting as a motivator of unethical behavior. *Academy of Management Journal, 47*(3), 422–432.

Simons, R. (1995a). Control in an age of empowerment. *Harvard Business Review, 73*(2) 80–81.

Simons, R. (1995b). *Levers of control, how managers use innovative control systems to drive strategic renewal.* Boston, MA: Harvard Business School Press.

Sivabalan, P., Booth, P., Malmi, T., & Brown, D. A. (2009). An exploratory study of operational reasons to budget. *Accounting & Finance, 49*(4), 849–871.

Statoil. (2010). *Statutory report 2010.* Retrieved from http://www.statoil.com/AnnualReport2010/en/Download%20Center%20Files/01%20Key%20Downloads/13%20Statutory%20report/Statutoryreport_2010.pdf

Stratton, A. (2006). Sierra Trucks: Implementing real activity-based budgeting. In T. C. Adkins (Ed.), *Case studies in performance management: A guide from the experts* (pp. 117–133). Hoboken, NJ: Wiley.

Stringer, C. (2007). Empirical performance management research: Observations from AOS and MAR. *Qualitative Research in Accounting & Management, 4*(2), 92–114.

Stringer, C. P. (2006). Performance management: An empirical study. Dunedin, New Zealand: University of Otago. Unpublished PhD Thesis.

Taylor, F. W. (1916). *The principles of scientific management.* New York, NY: Norton.

Vroom, V. H. (1964). *Work and motivation.* New York, NY: Wiley.

Yerkes, R. M., & Dodson, J. (1908, November). The relation of strength of stimulus to rapidity of habit formation. *Journal of Comparative Neurology and Psychology, 18*, 459–482.

Zimmerman, J. L. (2006). *Accounting for decision making and control* (5th ed.). New York, NY: McGraw-Hill.

Index

Note: *cc* denotes case capsule; *f,* figure; and *t,* table.

Announcing the Business Expert Press Digital Library

Concise E-books Business Students
Need for Classroom and Research

This book can also be purchased in an e-book collection by your library as
- a one-time purchase,
- that is owned forever,
- allows for simultaneous readers,
- has no restrictions on printing,
- can be downloaded as PDFs from within the library community.

Our digital library collections are a great solution to beat the rising cost of textbooks. E-books can be loaded into their course management systems or onto students' e-book readers.

The **Business Expert Press** digital libraries are very affordable, with no obligation to buy in future years.

For more information, please visit **www.businessexpertpress.com/librarians**. To set up a trial in the United States, please contact **Sheri Dean** at sheri.dean@globalpress.com; for all other regions, contact **Nicole Lee** at nicole.lee@igroupnet.com.

OTHER TITLES IN OUR MANAGERIAL ACCOUNTING COLLECTION

Collection Editor: **Kenneth A. Merchant**, *University of Southern California*

- *Corporate Investment Decisions: Principles and Practice* by Michael Pogue
- *Drivers of Successful Controllership: Activities, People, and Connecting with Management* by Jürgen Weber and Pascal Nevries
- *Revenue Management: A Path to Increased Profits* by Ronald Huefner
- *Cost Management and Control in Government: Fighting the Cost War Through Leadership Driven Management* by Dale Geiger
- *Breakeven Analysis: The Definitive Guide to Cost-Volume-Profit Analysis* by Michael Cafferky and Jon Wentworth
- *Revenue Management in Service Organizations* by Paul Rouse, Julie Harrison, and William Maguire

www.ingramcontent.com/pod-product-compliance
Lightning Source LLC
Chambersburg PA
CBHW071856200326
41519CB00016B/4402